and Healthy

What You Need to Know About Mental Health and Healthy Aging— for You and Your Loved Ones

MURALI RAO, MD, FACLP, DLFAPA
Professor & Chair, Department of Psychiatry
& Behavioral Neurosciences
Loyola University Chicago

50+ and Healthy: What You Need to Know about Mental Health and Healthy Aging—for You and Your Loved Ones

©2020 by Murali Rao

ISBN: 978-1-7351775-0-2 (paperback)

All rights reserved. This work may not be reproduced or translated in part or in whole without written permission. The designations employed and the presentation of the material in this publication do not imply the expression of any opinion whatsoever on the part of the authors concerning the legal status of any country, territory, city, or area or of its authorities, or concerning the delimitation of its frontiers or boundaries.

The mention of specific companies or products does not imply that they are endorsed or recommended by the authors in preference to others of a similar nature that are not mentioned. Errors and omissions excepted, the names of proprietary products are distinguished by initial capital letters.

All reasonable precautions have been taken by the authors to verify the information contained in this publication. However, the published material is being distributed without warranty of any kind, either expressed or implied. The responsibility for the interpretation and use of the material lies with the reader. In no event shall the authors be held liable for damages arising from its use.

An important note: This book is *not* intended as a substitute for the medical recommendation of physicians or other healthcare providers. Always consult with licensed health professionals. The identities of people described in the case histories have been changed to protect patient confidentiality.

Illustrations and photographs under license from DepositPhotos.com

Book layout and cover design by DTPerfect.com

"Age is an issue of mind over matter. If you don't mind, it doesn't matter."

—Mark Twain

Table of Contents

Part 1: What You Need to Know:
Facts about Mental Health and Mental Illness — 1

   What You Will Learn — 3

   Introduction — 5

   Chapter 1: The Research and Some Statistics — 13

   Chapter 2: What is Mental Health? — 25

   Chapter 3: What is Mental Illness? — 29

   Chapter 4: What Do We Mean By Healthy Aging? — 35

   Chapter 5: The Unnecessary Stigma around Mental Illness — 45

Part 2: Identifying & Understanding the Illnesses — 57

   Chapter 6: Identifying & Understanding Some Specific Mental Disorders — 59

   Chapter 7: Six Cases — 79

Part 3: Practical Approaches for First Aid and Later Interventions — 87

   Chapter 8: What You Control — 89

   Chapter 9: Do or Don't? — 99

   Chapter 10: Your GAME PLAN™ for Assisting Others in Distress — 105

   Chapter 11: Myth or Reality? — 109

Part 4: Your Own Healthy Aging — 119

   Chapter 12: Practical Approaches You Can Adopt — 121

   Conclusion — 127

Part 1

What You Need to Know — Facts about Mental Health and Mental Illness

What You Will Learn

This is an educational primer for a general public of learners possessing no particular knowledge in the area of mental health or mental illness.

Though the material is directed towards learning to help elders, the material can readily apply to any age group.

You will learn:

- What is meant by healthy aging, and by mental health vs. mental illness

- Some statistics around mental illness

- To understand/recognize what the various specific mental disorders are

- To understand some of the causes, risk factors and treatments of those disorders

- What to do to best assist an elder in a mental health crisis

- Lifestyle actions you can take to promote your own healthy aging

Introduction

To all my readers: Thank you for being willing to help others and yourself to maintain or regain your mental health through education. We cannot take action on something we do not understand, and how to preserve and improve mental health — and help those with mental disorders — is indeed something you can learn and understand.

I am Murali Rao, MD. My medical specialization is Geriatric (Elder) Psychiatry and Behavioral Neurosciences. I'm a professor, and chairman of Loyola University Medical Center's Department of Psychiatry and Behavioral Neurosciences.

My thrust in my daily work is with the elder (geriatric) population, but — and this is important — ***much of what I present herein can be applied to people of any age.***

There is much knowledge, easily accessible and fairly understandable, about regaining and maintaining your *physical* health. In fact, most people know more about the physical health aspects of self-care than they probably realize. Bring up the topic of mental health, however, and people seem to freeze up. Learning about mental illness and understanding actions to take that can support mental health will liberate you from that frozen state!

My job in this book is

A. to give you a general introductory background about mental health, and how/why mental illness may manifest itself.

B. to guide you in helping those elders around you who may be experiencing one or more of the mental disorders that you will be reading about.

C. to give you some tools to maintain your own good mental health and wellness as you yourself move into your elder years.

You won't need to be a 'science geek' or have any prior medical training to easily follow along. This book is by no means for the medical professional. It is for you who need knowledge that you can act upon — to help elders in your life, and prepare for your own healthy elder years. I'll leave the heavy research and the technical terms alone for the most part. I will, however, be speaking from a scientific, data-supported base of knowledge.

To help a mentally ill individual does not always require medical training, but it does require some knowledge and a mindset of openness.

Introduction

It's Personal

Just as the definition of 'living well' will be different from person to person, so too the definition of 'aging well' or 'healthy aging' is different from one individual to the next.

It's very personal!

What do you know about living healthfully — about healthy aging? What do you probably already know about physical illness versus mental illness as we age?

> Aging does not mean illness of either type is inevitable.
>
> Neither type of illness is 'good' or 'bad'. Both simply require attention, first from you yourself, then from a trained health professional.
>
> Any individual on the planet can experience both physical and mental illness, and they can be passing (short-lived, acute) or linger (longer-term, recurring, chronic).
>
> Either type is still an illness or disharmony of the holistic (entire mechanism of the) body, which can be aided by professional health care, advice, treatments.
>
> There are aspects of both types of health which are outside our personal control, yet there are many aspects within our direct and personal control.

Who Takes Care of Our Mental Health?

Mental Health is also known by the names of *Behavioral Health* and *Cognitive Health*. Although amongst mental health practitioners we give each a specific definition, I will be using them fairly interchangeably in this book for simplicity's sake.

There are a number of highly and specifically trained professions which focus on aspects of mental health and the treatment of mental illnesses.

Clinical Psychiatrist — Psychiatrists are first and foremost medical doctors. They are licensed physicians. A psychiatrist is generally the only professional who specializes in mental health care and can prescribe medications to treat mental disorders. Some psychiatrists provide psycho-therapy.

Clinical Psychologist — These professionals are not physicians but must hold a doctoral degree (PhD or PsyD). Psychologists receive long hours of specific training facing real patients — in diagnosis, psychological-cognitive-mental health assessment, and learn a wide variety of psychotherapies.

Other mental health professionals include:

- General Practice Physicians
- Psychiatric Nurses
- Psychiatric Technicians
- Clinical Social Workers
- Marriage and Family Counselors/Therapists
- Substance Abuse Counselors

Our Collective Knowledge about Mental Health

I will be presenting some statistic data and medically/scientifically-acquired evidence in the following chapter. Although research is constantly taking place around the world, alas, much of the current literature is still marked by its own authors as *inconclusive for a population as a whole*. This is due to many factors:

> A certain area of mental health research may still be in its infancy, particularly as in past research the focus was on mental *illness* while today there is more a trend to study mental *health* and what creates, recreates and sustains it.

> We have not tracked any large group of young participants' overall and specific mental health through all their years to their elder death. This means that research to date has tracked *either* the young or the elderly— not a group throughout their entire lifespan. There is thus a lack of individualized benchmarks for almost all study participants, whether healthy or already affected to a degree by the studied disorder. (i.e.: We don't yet have a study creating benchmarks of younger-year cognition, stress adaptation, resilience, environmental factors like nutrition and exercise, etc., that can be measured against their results in later years of the same study of the same individual). Researchers are understandably reluctant to extrapolate too far into a future or reach too far into the past of their study participants at the risk of ending up with subjective rather than objectively measured results.

- Mental health 'markers' and mental illness 'risk factors' — physical, mental/emotional, environmental, genetic, familial — are numerous and varied enough that the wide range of combinations of them makes each of us truly individual in the elder outcomes we will experience. For instance, researchers do not yet know why 10 autopsied females who showed no mental illness at any time during their lives — and notably no Alzheimer's Disease through their elder years — still held within their bodies clear markers for Alzheimer's Disease. What other factors within those women's control (or that we simply do not yet understand) were activated during their lifetimes such that the AD was itself not activated? We are individuals, and the combinations of causes and contexts can make it challenging to understand.

- Finally, there are factors outside our individual control and factors within our personal control.

  - Outside our control, at least for the present time, we have (in no particular order)

    - our genetic makeup

    - toxicity levels and types of our general environment (body, home, neighborhood/region)

    - choices made for us when we were young children (which may include subjection to abuse of various types, excellent/poor nutrition, availability/restriction of educational opportunity, regular/no family tradition of exercise or sport, presence/absence of a faith-based behavior set, etc.).

Within our control are the optimistic (or not) choices we make and healthful (or not) actions we take.

It is the exercise of that control (or not) that is so variable.

Even for individuals who know intellectually of their power to make beneficial changes, they can variously decide to take action on or ignore that information.

All this said, research has brought many significant trends to the light of day, and we can add those health-providing trends to our common-sensical daily routines, and to our arsenal of current medical tools, therapies and treatments, and begin to take care of ourselves as we and our loved ones age in a more health-producing fashion.

In the chapters following the (light and understandable, rest assured!) research, I will explain some of the most common mental disorders to help you not only identify and understand them in the elders around you, but to learn that treatments are available for all of them (and what those treatments or therapies are). Some disorders, as I have mentioned, will have aspects of treatment under the individual's own control — such as eating differently — while other types of treatment will require the intervention or consultation with a trained medical/mental health professional for best outcomes.

Self-Quiz

On each self-quiz in these pages, first do your best to answer without looking at the Answer Key that follows it. Of course, feel free to review the chapter's information as you go along. Then check your answers.

True or False?

1. ____ Healthy Aging means the same thing to everyone.

2. ____ You need to have some medical training to help an elder with mental illness.

3. ____ Medicine and science don't know much about mental illness and how to treat it.

4. ____ As we age, we will undoubtedly contract both physical and mental illnesses of some nature.

5. ____ The 'markers' of mental health and the 'risk factors' that lead to developing mental illness are known by medicine and researchers.

6. ____ Mental illnesses of any kind are the person's own fault and they should just snap out of it.

7. ____ 'Risk factors' potentially leading to mental disorders are in two categories: the ones in our personal control, and the ones we do not have control over.

1.F 2.F 3.F 4.F 5.T 6.F 7.T

Chapter 1

THE RESEARCH AND SOME STATISTICS

s in all learning, it is a good idea to have first the 'Big Picture' on the topic which we could say is at the top of the funnel, then to work your way down that funnel to more specific and detailed information.

Globally

What does the mental health picture look like on a world scale?

The World Health Organization (WHO) states, "***One in four people** in the world will be affected by <u>mental or neurological</u> disorders at some point in their lives. Around 450 million people currently suffer from such conditions, placing mental disorders among the leading causes of ill-health and disability worldwide.*" Note that these are numbers from 2001, and have increased since then.

One in four people, or ¼ of our globe's population, totals nearly <u>2 billion people</u>. 2 billion people who will — at some time in their child, teen or adult lives — experience mental disorders (or mental illness).

We have spent most of our past research efforts around the world on the mental disorders and mental illness. There is now a sea change in that international effort towards identifying what it is that can create or recreate and maintain mental *health*.

The WHO further states, "*Treatments are available, but **nearly two-thirds** of people with a known mental disorder **never seek help** from a health professional. <u>**Stigma, discrimination and neglect**</u> prevent care and treatment from reaching people with mental disorders. Where there is neglect, there is little or no understanding. **Where there is no understanding, there is neglect.**"

- 350 million worldwide are believed to suffer from major chronic depression in any given year of measure.

- An estimated 44 million people worldwide are afflicted with dementia, including Alzheimer's Disease in 2015, with some saying that the number could triple by 2050.

- The total estimated worldwide cost of dementia is US$818 billion in 2015, growing to over $1 trillion by 2018.

Dr Gro Harlem Brundtland, Director-General of WHO (World Health Organization), made the following statement upon releasing the World Health Report: "*Mental illness is **not***

a personal failure. *In fact, if there is failure, it is to be found in the way we have responded to people with mental and brain disorders."*

Again, the WHO has discovered that:

> More than 40% of countries have no mental health policies and over 30% have no mental health programs.
>
> Around 25% of countries have no mental health legislation.
>
> At this time, more than 33% of countries — or only about 75 countries out of all 192 nations — devote less than 1% of their total health budgets to mental health, with an equal number only spending 1% of their budgets on mental health.
>
> Although a limited range of medicines is sufficient to treat the majority of mental disorders, only ¼ of countries stock the three most commonly prescribed drugs used to treat schizophrenia, depression and epilepsy.
>
> There is only one psychiatrist per 100,000 people in over half the countries in the world.
>
> 40% of all nations have less than one hospital bed reserved for mental disorders per 10,000 patients.
>
> It is the poor shouldering the greater burden of mental disorders, both in terms of the risk in having

a mental disorder and the lack of access to treatment. They either have no nearby mental health services or cannot afford them.

The elderly demographic everywhere is particularly vulnerable. Their (often) multiple co-existing medical conditions (chronic or acute, e.g.: cardiovascular disease, respiratory limitations, hearing and visual impairments, infections) complicate not only accurate and complete diagnosis but effective treatment of mental health issues that arise.

The most common psychiatric problems among elders are depression, anxiety, dementia, and suicide.

Caregiver Burden: The Sandwich Generation

Are you from the Sandwich Generation? If you are raising your own children as well as caring for your elder parent (or grandparent) who can no longer care for himself — you are a member of the sandwich generation. The stress — emotional, mental and physical — is exacerbated by the stress of the clock. Time is not on our side as we try to balance care of self with care of minor children, and with care of parent (and perhaps grandparent). There are not enough hours in the day nor enough energy in your body to do it all, yet you have shouldered that burden nonetheless as "your family duty".

You are also part of the sandwich generation if you have adult children and find yourself not only being the 'designated babysitter' for your children's children, but for your parents.

And make no mistake, if you are one of these, you are also still trying to keep your head on your own job or career while adding that caregiving responsibility.

In our world's more traditional societies, the younger set has moved out of the family's generational village and into the cities. Even when the son has the traditional financial burden of parental care, the daughter has the physical caregiving role. Yet that is changing around the world. Traditional caregiving practices are gone from most modern societies now too (whether in Japan, India, Hawaii, Norway or New York): It is a fact that all children have long since preferred to pursue an advanced education and that good salary in the distant city to staying at home with his/her infirm elder parent for years of 'unfulfilling' (and unpaid) care. It is often, too, a fact that the son must go to the city to even find a paying job that will pay for parental care.

The family nucleus and the traditional practice of having many children so that they provide/care for us in our elder years has been lost to the pure economics of survival. The jobs are in the cities. Mother and Father raised us in the country - and they raised us to be independent. We have, especially over the past generation, lost sight of the fact that illness in elder years robs us of that independence. The stress and burden is real on many fronts.

India is the world's third largest economy. Yet it is no different from, say, California in the US (the world's fifth largest economy), in that caring for elders presents a real societal and family dilemma. Even if a sufficient number of assisted living facilities existed and were affordable to those who need them, can we afford it emotionally for our parent? Will they still feel we have abandoned them to alone-ness and separation from family for the rest of their years — in spite of the great daily care we have assured for them? Are we shirking our moral responsibility to our elders when we (albeit lovingly and with best intention) move them into a care facility that is far from the hubbub and interaction of loved family? Does the greater family lose some of its natural richness when the generations are separate? And yet, how can we make our home their own when we are not professional caregivers and they require more care than many young children - or when we are not medically knowledgeable about their needs and might make a disastrous decision for them?

These are stressful questions to ask, and just as heart-wrenching to answer and act upon.

In our homes and hearts, we do not need to measure our stress. It is ever-present. We feel sadness at our elder's illness. We simultaneously hope for an improvement in their condition. We grieve their passing during their living years. We juggle our budgets so that everything is covered as best we can. Maybe we have given up our hobbies or leisure (and this might deplete us) to carve out the time to spend with our elder. We just feel it, go with it, and manage the best we can.

But what we as caregivers must not ever forget is to take care of ourselves. In my profession, it is called 'respite' — time away from the intensity of caregiving that you spend on yourself and to recharge. Later chapters will give some clear guidelines on how to do that for yourself. It is only when you are well that you are able to be there for your elder loved one. Gaining information (as you are with this book) is a vital step, and developing a network of helpers is also beneficial as it takes some of the time and energy burden off your shoulders.

Data Specific to the United States of America

Let's move down the information funnel now, specifically looking at the United States and its contexts.

The overall population of the USA is 327,200,000 — of which nearly 15% or about 48 million people are aged 65 or older (2018).

> About one in five Americans, or 20%, experience mental illness in any given year.

> A mental illness will interfere with life and work for about 1 in 25 Americans each year.

Now let's break that down into specific mental diagnoses for the larger US population. You will learn more about each type of disorder in the next chapters of this book. For 2018:

> 1.1% of adults in the U.S. live with schizophrenia; that's over 3 million individuals.

> 2.6% of adults in the U.S. live with bipolar disorder.

> Nearly 7% of adults in the U.S., or about 16 million individuals, had at least one major depressive episode in the past year.

- 18.1% of adults in the U.S. experienced an anxiety disorder such as posttraumatic stress disorder, obsessive-compulsive disorder and specific phobias.

- Among the 20.2 million adults in the U.S. who experienced a substance use/abuse disorder, 50.5% or 10,200,000 adults, had a co-occurring mental illness.

- Only 41% of adults in the U.S. with a mental health condition received mental health services in the past year.

- Among adults with a serious mental illness, less than 63% received mental health services in the past year.

Identifiable Diagnoses

Now let's move down the funnel one last time to examine the situation within each identifiable illness.

Cognitive Disorders

Dementia. This is not a specific disorder, but a spectrum of cognitive reductions.

Alzheimer's Disease (AD) is one aspect of dementia. It is a progressive disease starting with minor memory loss, potentially moving to loss of the ability to carry on a conversation and respond to the environment.

Subjective Cognitive Decline (SCD) is a self-reported decline in memory or the frequency in memory loss or mental confusion, and seen as a precursor to Alzheimer's or dementia.

In 2014, an estimated 5 million Americans aged 65 years or older had Alzheimer's disease, and projected to rise to 14 million people by 2060.

The number of people living with the disease doubles every 5 years beyond age 65.

Depression

Some estimates of major chronic depression in older Americans living their usual lives in a community setting range from 1%-5%, increasing to 11.5% in older hospitalized patients, and to 13.5% in those receiving home healthcare.

Depression is more common in people who also have other illnesses: about 80% of older adults have at least one chronic physical health condition, and 50% have two or more.

Much depression goes entirely undiagnosed (no physician or mental health professional is ever consulted) or is misdiagnosed.

When diagnosed, depression is often untreated or undertreated.

The vast majority of individuals with mental illness continue to function in their daily lives. However:

nearly one in five (19-20 percent) U.S. adults experience some form of mental illness.

one in 24 (4.1 percent) has a serious mental illness.

- one in 12 (8.5 percent) has a diagnosable substance use disorder.

Suicide

Mental illness can manifest as suicidal talk to others or internal suicidal thoughts, suicide attempts (meaning real tries but which failed, with or without full recovery from the attempt) and suicides which have succeeded.

- In 2017, 47,000 Americans died by suicide.

- The same year there were 1.4 million attempted suicides (failures).

- Suicide is the number one cause of death for young people aged 10 to 35 (2017). This is America's highest suicide rate since World War II.

Nutrition

Nutrition — meaning food and beverage of good nutritional quality and sufficient caloric quantity — is a key determinant for holistic (i.e. overall) health and quality-of-life for all of us, but it is even more important in the older person.

- Up to 70% of elders hospitalized for a period of time may be at nutritional risk — under-hydrated and/or malnourished (insufficient nutrients) or undernourished (insufficient calories and/or nutrients).

- The number is still a high 60% for newly hospitalized geriatric patients.

CHAPTER 1: THE RESEARCH AND SOME STATISTICS

Contrary to younger individuals, elders don't bounce back quickly from under-nutrition caused by illness, unavailability of food, depression or dementia.

They don't bounce back easily from a weight loss or a loss of muscle capacity/strength.

A vicious cycle sets in of loss of appetite/anorexia, physical weakness or chronic inflammatory processes.

If this data tells us nothing else, it is that mental illnesses affect people around the globe and across our own country. It tells us that we need to take its diagnosis and treatment seriously, and that no one seems 'immune', so to speak, from experiencing some degree and form of mental illness in his/her lifetime.

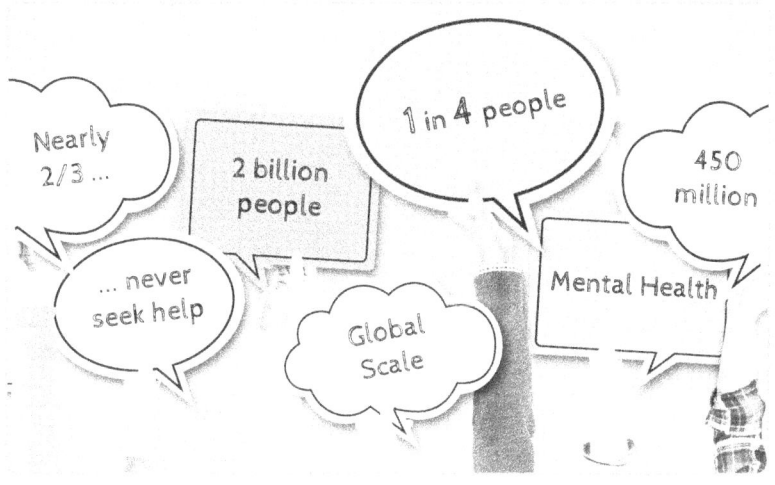

WHAT IS MENTAL HEALTH?

sk any three mature adults who say "I'm healthy" what they mean by that, and you will get three different answers. One will say "I don't need any prescription drugs", another "I am never sick and I don't have any aches or pains", and the third boasts that "Everything still works!"

For the layman, when it comes to discussions of 'good health', especially good mental health, we leave the zone of measurable parameters and objectivity and enter into a subjective zone. In mental health, the professionals are faced with the challenge of 'standardization'.

Standardization is a tool physicians can use to objectively measure one individual against a wide population. As an example in a physical health scenario, we have long since developed 'standardized, acceptable ranges' for *blood cholesterol*. That is, there is a range of blood cholesterol amounts, from low to high, within which we say we are healthy. Below that amount or above it, we are advised to take medically-guided corrective action to restore health.

But how do we measure a person's *memory recall*? Indeed, it may not seem easy to measure cognition or mental capabilities in our older years, except in relation to what we experienced in our younger ones. Standardization, objective measurement, is out the window.

Defining Mental Health

Here is what the World Health Organization says about Mental Health:

> It is "*a state of wellbeing in which the individual realizes his or her own abilities, can cope with the normal stresses of life, can work productively and fruitfully, and is able to make a contribution to his or her community.*"

Mental health is the basis for emotions/feelings, thinking, communication, learning, resilience (ability to bounce back from stresses and all types of setbacks) and self-esteem/self-confidence.

Mental health is also key to developing relationships and interacting socially, to personal and emotional well-being, to contributing out in the world and at home.

Mental Health allows effective functioning in daily activities. We thus experience:

- productivity in tasks and activities we perform (in working, schooling, caregiving) healthy, mutually-beneficial relationships

adaptability to change, both planned and spontaneous

ability to cope with/bounce back from stresses, setbacks, adversity

Chapter 3

WHAT IS MENTAL ILLNESS?

Identifying a state called mental illness may or may not truly be an objective exercise. What we observe in ourselves and those we are close with is one or more signals or symptoms of *decline* or *change* in mental functioning, a decline or change from the prior, younger years 'normal'. And it is not always — far from it — a sign of mental illness.

Defining Mental Illness

The American Psychiatric Association defines mental illness this way:

> *"Mental illnesses are health conditions involving changes in emotion, thinking or behavior (or a combination of these). Mental illnesses are associated with distress and/or problems functioning in social, work or family activities."*

'Mental illness' thus indeed is a matter of observed changes. Mental or cognitive or behavioral illnesses are not all one thing. As in physical ailments, they are a number of diagnosable and separately distinguishable mental, cognitive or behavioral disorders.

Identifiable and Treatable

There are some specific mental disorders that we will look at in the next part of the book. For now, what are a few characteristics of mental or cognitive or behavioral illness?

NOTE: Please keep in mind that this list is not about a single identifiable mental illness, but represents a spectrum of changes in an individual which may indicate the onset/presence of an identifiable mental disorder.

- Trouble remembering. E.g.: not remembering who people are, or where we placed a certain much-used item in our home, or forgetting written appointments.

- An observable change in behaviors or in expression of emotions. E.g.: acting notably more erratic or suddenly more subdued.

- Loss of attention in its different forms. E.g.: inability to sustain attention on a subject or project.

- Trouble in what we call executive functioning — our capacity to plan, organize, oversee or monitor behaviors that are purposefully directed. E.g.: taking steps to achieve a goal or complete a project.

- Losing touch with reality. Hallucinating. Acting unfamiliar (unsettled) with a formerly familiar place or space or environment.

- Stumbling with language functions. E.g.: an inability to find the word we were looking for, produce correct word sequences.

- A reduction in usual mental processing speed. Processing speed is the time it takes us to absorb a given amount of information.

In self-observation, we'll find ourselves to often saying things like, "I'm having a senior moment here" when memory fails us, or "I didn't used to be this slow at _____" when referring to a mental operation.

For most of us, it is our 'decline' or that 'change' we perceive, as loosely compared in our minds to the prior, accustomed 'normal' and healthy capabilities. We see that we are no longer at our personal 'normal', but performing at somewhat less than that. Since a personal 'normal' is just that — personal — it is difficult to standardize across a population.

The APA reminds us that mental health conditions are identifiable (that means a physician can correctly diagnose them) and treatable. Just like a physical illness, they are nothing to be ashamed or embarrassed about — not by the person affected by it, and not by the people close to the affected person (family, caregivers, friends, therapists, etc.).

Health and Illness

A person experiencing good mental health feels in control of his emotions and behavioral choices, has a good cognitive (i.e.: mental/intellectual) function and generally positive interactions with the people around him and the events of his world. A person with a mental illness may have difficulty or new inability with some or all of this.

Being in a good state of mental health, an individual can take care of himself, perform in work/social situations, develop harmonious relationships. A person with a mental illness may withdraw or isolate, may not recognize people he's long known, may become unable to interact with them as before.

Being in a state of mental health and wellness, a person can cope on his own with passing stresses and with passing negative emotions such as sadness, anger or jealousy (or ensure that they do not linger). Large or small stresses, or sudden changes of any type, may be beyond the ability of a mentally ill individual to deal with.

Good physical health is not the absence of physical illness nor just the absence of pain or other negative symptoms alone — but a measure of good body responsiveness to outside stimuli, a sense of comfort and wellbeing and energy, a sense of physical alertness and vitality, a sense of personal control and independence.

Likewise, mental *health* is not just the absence of mental *illness*.

Self-Quiz

True or False?

Don't look at the Answer Key, but review the previous two chapters' material to answer these questions. Then consult the Answer Key that follows.

1. ____ In mental health assessments and testing, there are few 'standardized, acceptable ranges'.

2. ____ Mental health disorders are not identifiable, nor are they treatable to any degree by modern medicine.

3. ____ A decline in memory is one of the early ways we can recognize 'cognitive decline'.

4. ____ It is easy for a medical professional to compare an elder patient's cognitive function with his younger-year capability.

5. ____ Mental health is the basis for emotions/feelings, the ability to bounce back from stresses and all types of setbacks - among others.

6. ____ This is an accurate description of mental illness: "Mental illnesses are health conditions involving changes in emotion, thinking or behavior (or a combination of these). Mental illnesses are associated with distress and/or problems functioning in social, work or family activities."

1.T 2.F 3.T 4.F 5.T 6.T

What Do We Mean By Healthy Aging?

We've looked at health versus illness, and we move between the two during our entire lifetime, with, hopefully most of our time spent in a state of health. In times past, we thought of aging as *necessarily including* both physical and mental decline. We saw them going hand in hand in the elderly. We know today that is not the case.

More and more, the definition of 'healthy aging' will revolve around the brain's health and around cognitive/mental and emotional health of the individual in his world — as it evolves in close relationship to one's physical health.

In prior times, aging healthfully might have only meant a person's outstanding physical health and wellness as measured against accepted 'standard ranges' in one's lab tests like bloodwork, and through specific physical exams. Today, we join the two aspects: Healthy aging means good physical health and good mental health.

The field of psychiatry and psychology emerged in the early 20th century. More than one hundred years later, there are still no 'standard ranges' that everyone agrees upon to measure 'healthy mental aging', as I stated earlier. But we have collected much useful information about mental and emotional health and illness — and devised treatments (protocols or therapies) for them.

Healthy aging might be described as:

1. freedom from disabilities and disease
2. a responsive physical body
3. a responsive mental cognition
4. a balanced emotional state of being, without dramatic high or low moods or behaviors
5. a capacity for social engagement, including conversation and interaction with multiple people (as opposed to withdrawal from society)

All elders, wherever we are in the world, value our physical and cognitive independence, which we typically describe as the ability to live alone and care for ourselves without the help of other individuals, and the capability of 'paying our own way' or not being a burden on others.

In more traditional cultures, this type of independence might not be as important as connection to one's immediate and extended family — living with family, having a role to perform within the family circle even as one ages, etc.

How Old Do You Feel?

"If you didn't know how old you were, how old would you be?"

This parlor game question summarizes the fact that we don't have any single set of biomarkers to represent our biological age (when the number of years since our birth is our 'chronological' age). *"You are as old as you feel"* is thus probably the closest answer we have today, with healthy 80-year-olds stating they don't feel different from their 30s (and unhealthy 40-year-olds saying they feel like they are 90)! Do you see again how personal aging well can be?

More today than ever, we would rather increase the number of <u>healthy</u> years that we live rather than arbitrarily living to be a centenarian but ignoring health and wellness.

That is where we are at with defining successful physical aging — it remains a rather subjective evaluation for most of us.

What Is Healthy Aging?

Simply put, 'physical' health, 'cognitive' or 'mental' health and 'emotional' or 'behavioral' health collectively represent how we experience life from our bodies and minds. This collective health means we can act and interact in our world in a harmonious, independent manner.

Healthy cognitive and emotional aging means more than the <u>absence</u> of depression and anxiety or other disorder. Health in this context might mean the ability to

- self-regulate/manage one's emotions — an emotional self-control
- the presence of contentment and happiness, natural optimism and a positive outlook
- mastery/control over one's behaviors
- a sense of control over one's world, one's personal affairs

Like physical health, a number of factors are involved to create mental health. Whether we like it or not, the data and research show that ...

- a high educational attainment
- a prosperous socio-economic life
- the habit of physical activity, and
- residing in a harmonious, caring environment
- being intellectually/socially curious and active

... all contribute to later-life mental health. Is it because education or these other components create a reserve, as it were, to draw upon during times of stress, allowing us to easily and quickly bounce back from a passing depression or moment of anxiety? Again we enter a zone of subjectivity.

Mental and Emotional Reserves

Research has been undertaken on the existence and the effects of 'brain reserves' as well as 'emotional reserves' in relation to later-life mental health.

The first is still little known, and the starting premise is that — just as some people simply have greater muscular strength throughout their lives than others — brain strength or brain capacity is also different from one person to another. Does this brain reserve help to create or sustain later-life mental health? Stay tuned for more research results.

Emotional reserves, like that greater muscular strength, is also a later-life resource to maintain mental health. These reserves are what allow some of us to deal head on with (and fairly quickly resolve and move on from) life's challenges, troubles, shocks and stresses — while others of us wallow in them, wring our hands, get and stay emotional and reactive for quite a longer time.

An ability to self-motivate and take one's overall health in charge might be part of that emotional reserve, and it goes a long way to maintaining one's physical, emotional and mental health. This might include self-monitoring, since major depression and dementia evolve slowly, over years and decades. Recognizing a 'minor' cognitive decline or 'mild' or 'sporadic' emotional issues early on can help the individual combat more severe mental disorders very early. (The "nip it in the bud" approach.)

Mental Attitude

Moving to something for which the research has clearer results, we look at the power of being positive. It is fairly easy for us to determine whether another individual has a positive or a negative outlook. Here is where mind meets emotions: We see and feel it!

Characteristics of a cheerful, positive disposition:

A. enthusiastic support for others' endeavors

B. expressions of happiness and joy with one's life

C. the ability to make lemonade out of lemons definitely represent a positive outlook

Conversely, negativity arises in the form of:

A. expressed or suppressed anger, fear, sadness

B. constant complaining or rude gossiping

C. jealousy of others' accomplishments

D. a doomsday outlook for one's future

E. a 'what's the use?' outlook

There's no confusing the two sets of emotions as they are polar opposites. Research and studies have long shown that individuals with largely positive emotions/feelings and optimistic outlooks are more likely to be healthy in all ways than those who hold and express largely pessimistic, negative feelings/emotions and unhappy views of their lives and their world. The positive individuals tend to cope and adapt quicker and more effectively than the negative ones to challenges, bad news or crises.

Emotions create/support physical health or they create/perpetuate illness.

>feelings such as chronic anger or hostility can increase coronary heart disease risk factors

>anxiety disorder has been associated with greater physical disability and diminished well-being

>depression is connected to a lesser health and lower quality of life, and a greater risk for death from suicide or medical illness

Emotions are a very real component of our physical, emotional, social, spiritual, mental/cognitive health.

Measuring Cognition

Mental cognition involves other types of functions, which mental health professionals measure:

>Fluid intelligence, as expressed in problem-solving and inductive reasoning (operations independent of context and content)

>Retentive memory

>Attention, or the time span of attention and focus on a range of things

>Language functions, including finding your words

>Executive functions, which is planning and rapid decision-making ability

>Speed of mental processing

- Social cognition, such as maintaining one or more good relationships
- Expressing sympathy/empathy appropriately

Measuring cognition in the elderly, although it is widely done, is challenging as I have stated. The reason measuring such cognition is challenging is due to the presence of undetected as well as known health conditions (arthritis, dehydration, some types of medication, metabolic conditions, early-stage undiagnosed chronic disease) which can all impact cognition to greater or lesser degrees.

Self-Quiz
True or False?

1. ____ In the past, 'healthy aging' just meant having good physical health and the ability to get around on one's own.

2. ____ Today, aging means we must lose our physical health and develop some sort of mental disorder as well. It's inevitable — that is what aging is!

3. _____ Psychiatry and psychology are brand new to the 21st century, so they really don't have any solutions for mental illness yet.

4. _____ Being a centenarian means you have perfect physical and mental health.

5. _____ Healthy emotional and mental (also called cognitive) aging only means being free of chronic depression and never feeling anxious.

6. _____ Smart, well-educated people enjoy mental health at all ages. Poverty and lack of education are major factors in developing mental illness.

7. _____ Negative emotions are well-known factors in creating and/or perpetuating bad physical and poor mental health.

8. _____ Diagnosis or measurement of mental disorders is complicated by the presence of hidden and/or known physical health issues.

1. T 2. F 3. F 4. F 5. F 6. F 7. T 8. T

THE UNNECESSARY STIGMA AROUND MENTAL ILLNESS

imply recognizing and treating a mental illness represents definite challenges to any patient. Adjustments to lifestyle, personal environment, activities and so on can be daunting to admit and to make.

As we have seen in the statistics and will see later in the Case Studies chapter, the challenge of access to professional mental health treatment is real in all our nations. Probably all the challenges seem insurmountable until the individual has begun some consultation, treatment or a care protocol, and has made a few adjustments at home.

Stigma Around Dementia

Let's use 'dementia' as an example of how stigma might be expressed. Dementia is a term for a number of mental disorders, of which Alzheimer's Disease is the dominant form we see (about 60% of cases of dementia). There is a particularly strong stigma around dementia. **Externally**, the stigma is expressed through rejection and fear of the person with the disorder and of his symptoms and new and unpredictable behaviors. Family and life-long friends start staying away — no longer extending invitations, not doing activities that were long done together, not including the person in conversation and so on. In short, this social and familial rejection hurts and might exacerbate the condition. It leads to social isolation. **Internally**, the stigma is expressed through mental confusion and emotional shame about having the disease and the uncontrollability of its symptoms. Fear of being alone for the rest of one's days goes hand-in-hand with the apparent opposite state of being dependent on others forevermore.

As with other expressions of stigma, education and information about dementia is the most effect approach to eliminating the stigma and beginning to get the help and support you need.

Stigma *around any form of mental illness* should not be one of the challenges anyone has to deal with.

External Stigma

A 'stigma' is defined in the Cambridge Dictionary as *'a strong disapproval; a strong lack of respect for someone or a bad opinion of them because they have done something society does not approve of'*.

In some of our societies, a (minor-aged or adult) unwed female who is pregnant is shunned — she is stigmatized, outcast. In other cultures, any divorced individual is stigmatized (and indeed was and may still be in some religious faiths).

Chapter 5: The Unnecessary Stigma around Mental Illness

Thus, being stigmatized by others is a sort of discrimination or exclusion which evolves from prejudiced/erroneous notions, beliefs or attitudes people have about your condition.

Mental illness is also stigmatized in most societies. It a deeply-seated attitude that most people cannot rationalize, yet still hold onto. It is a negative or discriminatory attitude, a preconceived notion that the mental illness of any individual is dangerous to others. Like much discrimination, it might come from a total lack of information (or wrong information) about mental illnesses in general or about specific mental disorders.

In society, the common fear is that individuals with mental health problems represent danger to others. These mental health disorders might include schizophrenia, bipolar disorder, alcoholism and drug dependency.

Other social stigma comes from a generally held belief that some mental health issues are self-created, they are the affected person's own fault and that, somehow, the person wants to have the illness. These types of behavioral/mental health issues might include eating disorders like bulimia or anorexia, or substance abuse (drugs or alcohol).

The behaviors of others arising from this stigma are their

    expressions/attitudes of distrust

    pity or shaming, guilt-tripping

    showing fear or dislike

- avoiding or rejecting the individual
- gossiping about the person from no factual knowledge of his/her condition
- assumptions that the individual with the illness is now very dangerous and one must stay clear of them
- that the mentally ill individual can no longer be reasoned with, you cannot talk to them
- that the individual is faking it
- is an easy mark for bullying, teasing or contempt
- is possessed by demons (as was much feared in past centuries)

There is a clear misunderstanding that people with mental disorders cannot be approached, are hard to talk to, and cannot be reasoned with (especially when it comes to seeking care), and that they are resistant to getting treatment. These notions are largely untrue.

Internal or Self-Stigma

This misunderstanding might come from another sort of stigma — an internalized, self-perceived stigma around one's own mental disorder. The internal stigma may stir up feelings of embarrassment, shame, false pride ("I can't let anyone see me like this; I'm not normal anymore."). Self-stigma might keep the individual from seeking factual knowledge about the disorder, keep him from seeking and following through with professional treatment and getting the support that is available either in the community at large or from the mental health community.

From the comments and attitudes of others, the ill person may begin to beat himself up and believe that it is indeed his fault. Expressions by others that the person with chronic depression disorder is just lazy, unmotivated to participate/perform in society or in the home, and is 'faking it' to get out of his/her responsibilities — these are burdens for the mentally ill person that he should not have to deal with.

The younger the individual with mental illness, i.e. a youngster of school age, the more likely he is to experience this external stigm from his own family members, classmates or teachers — and the self-stigma sets in. In other words, the negative attitudes and behaviors they perceive come from people they had hoped to be able to trust and receive support from in times of need. This leads younger individuals to lose a friend who walks away from fear or disgust or other feeling of dislike, or to unilaterally cut themselves off from friends and other family members and peers.

In our elder years, this self-stigma has a different source: We fear most losing our independence, and often our privacy. If we have been mobile and actively managing our own worldly affairs, it is a shock to no longer be able to take care of ourselves and get around on our own. If we have had a nice network of friends and family, we are concerned that now we will be a burden on them, or some of them, or that they will simply abandon us to our destiny. If we have been able to pursue our interests freely, but now cannot, we feel shackled — a prisoner of our mental incapacity.

Unfortunately, and as a medical doctor I have to be honest about this, there is some stigma against mental illness among medical professionals too — among those who are not trained in mental health specifically, but also those who otherwise do not prioritize mental health as part of a total or holistic health (body, mind, spirit) picture.

You wouldn't 'beat up on' a person just because she has a broken arm — no medical person would blame a patient for having such an injury. Why beat up on her for having any other type of illness — emotional, mental or physical?

This specific stigma against mental illness has been around for millennia and can be associated with our very present human fear or distrust of anyone or anything different from ourselves. Humans' very most basic need is to always seek to keep themselves safe and secure. We intuitively develop a comfort zone around us — a buffer of known people, familiar habits and traditions, familiar interactive behaviors and ways of doing things. If we are honest, this comfort zone constitutes our definition of 'normal'. Anything outside our 'normal' is to be feared, killed off, or at least we keep our distance and carefully watch how things develop. We see this every day in all aspects of our lives.

The stigma of mental illness goes deeper in our societies than you might think. Not just 'people' but 'institutions' express this discrimination:

governments

large and small health insurance companies

workplace health plans

workplace owners and managers

All fall short in acknowledging the need for comprehensive mental health education, authorized workplace health leaves, and mental health care coverage.

Health insurance policies (when they exist) have become so expensive for individuals and households that it has become trendy to piecemeal insurance coverage together according to one's budget, rather than one's potential needs. This typically leaves mental health coverage out in the cold. However, even when your policy allows mental health services, they are not always 'authorized' for coverage. Just one example among hundreds of institutional expressions of the stigma against mental health:

> *In a major class action lawsuit against United Behavioral Health (a large health insurer in the US), the insurance company was held liable for denying mental health benefits that were part of the policy they had issued.*

Fear of Change

Humans also resist any type of change — we resist changing from a junk food to a healthy food diet; we resist learning a new process in the workplace; we resist being told how to dress or behave. We resist because the way we are now is so comfortable! It requires little effort of us.

We resist mental illness because it throws us out of our comfort zone and outside our 'normal'. Mental illness we observe in others might be fearsome: It stirs up a fear that we ourselves might change from our 'normal' selves and contract the same illness. No longer being 'normal' is very scary to us.

In our day and age, the media plays a role in the perpetuating this fear and the stigma, but it may just as well (if we use it to this end) play a role in eradicating it. We see mental illness in our entertainment (films, television shows, books — and all the characters they may represent as homicidal, radically out of touch with reality, dangerously or violently mentally ill). It has to be said: Many of the portrayals are inaccurate and based on misinformation. However, they are there before us, cementing in our false, misinformed fears and disapprovals.

Why is the stigma against mental illness a public health concern?

First and foremost, it prevents the federal and local authorities and the ill individuals themselves from seeking professional care and treatment from a mental health practitioner that he can trust. He will resist coercive attempts to consult a professional; he is less likely to seek it on his own.

Secondly, and equally important, the stigma is often based on misinformation (or no knowledge whatsoever of the disorder), much less of the individual's environment and context.

Public education campaigns have proven valuable in changing people's minds about mental illness.

Thirdly, in the affected individual the stigma can create an emotional/mental downward spiral into despair, hopelessness, deeper depression, more acting out, more isolation. In short, the illness may be exacerbated.

Lastly, because of the negativity surrounding mental illness, the affected individual may not want to speak about their symptoms or needs, may resist finding supportive listeners to guide them to professional treatment, not seek factual information about the disorder — none of which is conducive to the individual willingly seeking and benefiting from the help that is available.

It is important in our societies, with such a well-identified presence of mental illnesses, to reduce negative stereotypes and increase our base of factual mental illness/mental health knowledge among the population at large. It is important, albeit difficult at first, to hold supportive and understanding attitudes toward people with mental illness.

Mentally ill individuals struggle doubly hard: first, with the illness or disability itself, then with the attached stigma. It is in our hands to reduce and eradicate the stigma in favor of support.

Self-Quiz

True or False?

1. ____ Disapproving of or fearing anyone's mental illness is human nature.

2. ____ 'Stigmatizing' someone is a sort of discrimination or exclusion of him.

3. ____ Most people have not thought through or rationalized why they feel fear or disapproval of mentally ill people and/or mental disorders.

4. ____ Anyone with bipolar disorder is really dangerous to others.

5. ____ The stigma against mental illness has been around for millennia.

6. ____ Alcoholism is not a mental illness, but comes from the person's own lack of self-control.

7. ____ Guilt-tripping someone for feeling deeply depressed is a form a stigmatization.

8. ____ Schizophrenics are possessed by demons, and that is a good reason to reject them from society.

9. ____ Stigma only comes from other people rejecting or shunning you.

10. ____ Personal shame about, or trying to hide, one's own mental disorder is a form of self-stigma.

11. ____ The stigma around mental illness can be lessened or eliminated through factual information and education.

1. T 2. T 3. T 4. F 5. T 6. F 7. T 8. F 9. F 10. T 11. T

Part 2

Identifying & Understanding the Illnesses

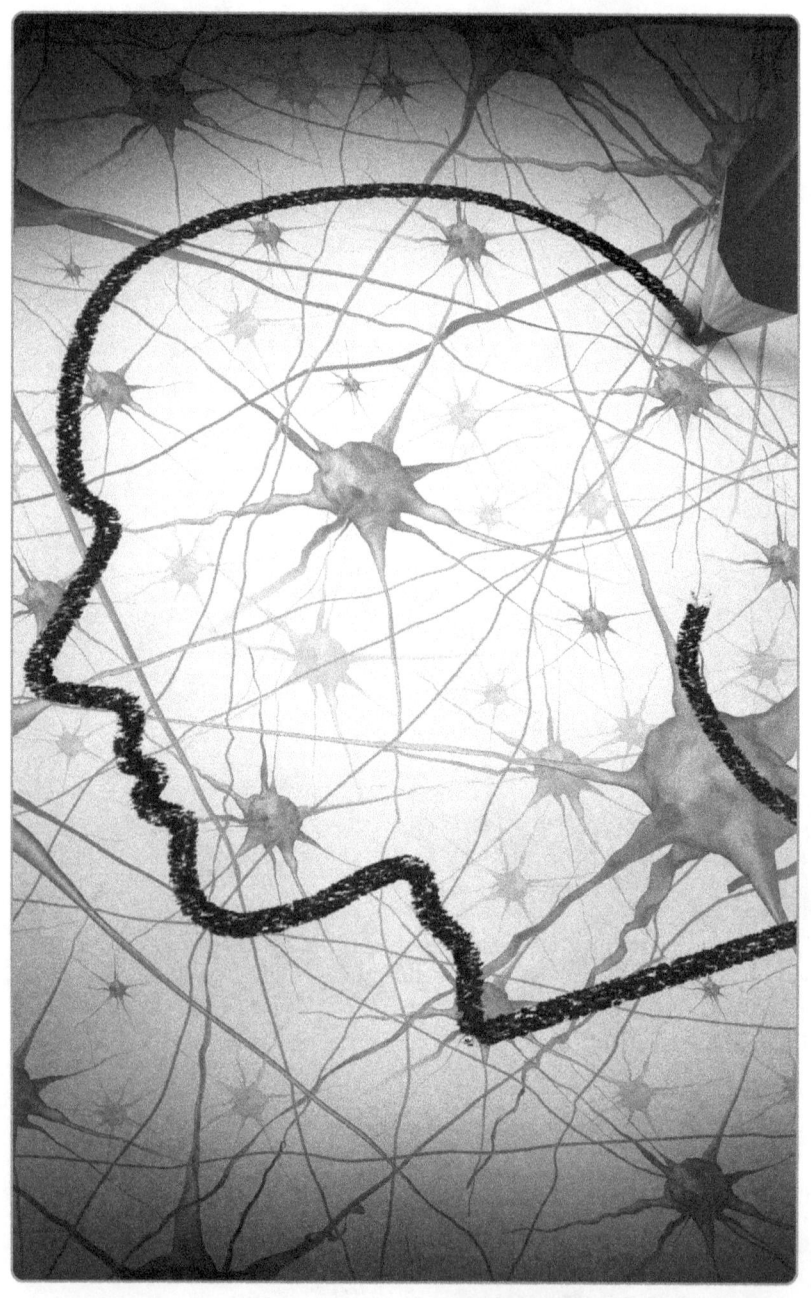

Chapter 6

IDENTIFYING & UNDERSTANDING SOME SPECIFIC MENTAL DISORDERS

> *NOTE: This chapter paints a broad, general picture of each disorder. Accurate, detailed and full diagnosis and choice of treatment by any mental health professional is necessarily specific to each patient, as there is (as already discussed) a great deal of personal context that must be taken into account.*

People who have a mental illness do not want to talk about it. Nor do the loved ones or close circle of people around them want to bring up the topic.

In fact, as we have just seen, people around someone with a mental disorder might stigmatize him, make him feel guilty or ashamed or embarrassed. Eradication of the hurtful social and familial stigma means breaking through the myths and the age-old patterns (guilt, shame, embarrassment, ostracism — for self, loved one or stranger).

Why? Because mental illness is nothing to be ashamed of! Not ever! Think of it as it truly is: a _medical condition_ or a _health condition_ — just like heart disease or diabetes. Like heart disease or high blood pressure, it can receive an accurate diagnosis and benefit from one or more known treatments.

The population as a whole is or will be directly or indirectly touched by the presence of mental illness — either personally or in a loved one. You owe it to them and to yourself to get informed and educated about not only the disorder itself (or several, if that is the case) but the various actions to take in the home on your own, and the various professionals and treatments that are available.

Mental illness — like physical illness and injury — does not discriminate. Anyone can be afflicted, and everyone who is afflicted can benefit from treatment.

The Forms It Takes

Physical disease, injury and illnesses take on many forms as we know. They range from a 2-week common cold to long-term chronic disease like diabetes to a sports injury like a broken bone.

Mental illness also takes on many forms. It manifests in degrees ranging from very mild to so severe that a person may need care in a hospital or specialist facility. It may seem to be 'only' an emotional disorder, and many will qualify depression or anxiety disorders as emotional. It may seem to be 'only' brain- or cognition-related, as in dementia, memory loss or mental confusion disorders. It may seem to be a combination of things, either simultaneously or alternately, such as anxiety hand-in-hand with dementia, or depression for a while followed by its opposite manic euphoria for a while (as in bipolar disorder).

Mild forms may 'gently bother' you in various aspects of your life and living, while the more severe manifestations pull you out of life's normal interactions and experiences. They are viewed and rightly so as passing phenomena.

Some forms of mental illness are better understood by the general public than others. For instance, virtually everyone has had an experience with anxiety, worry or fear (even panic), and can more or less explain what that felt like at the time. Likewise, any mature adult has probably experienced a time of sadness, grief or 'the blues' although it may not have qualified as major depression, but rather only a passing experience, soon resolved.

The descriptions and definitions of mental disorders which follow include an overview of:

- Alzheimer's Disease
- Anxiety
- Bipolar disorder
- Cognitive impairment
- Confusion
- Dementia

- Depression
- Panic attacks
- Psychosis
- Schizophrenia
- Suicidal thoughts/behaviors

These mental illnesses might be exacerbated or brought on earlier in life by the presence of a specific physical disease, by poor overall physical health. They can be worsened by an addiction (alcoholism, drug abuse). Addictions affect mental, emotional and physical health in different ways. Again, it is personal and the mental health professional will be the detective discovering all the causes and ramifications.

Depression & Bipolar Disorder

<u>Major Depressive Disorder</u> is a type of mood disorder. Qualifying as 'major' means that the episode lasts at least two weeks. It comes to disrupt a person's typically-performed daily activities or work routine. It may affect relationships due to the person's mood change. Major depressive disorder can be part of another illness called <u>Bipolar Disorder</u> (formerly called <u>Manic Depressive Disorder</u>).

Signs/symptoms of major depressive disorder: an unusually depressed, low, apathetic, low-energy mood

- lack of interest or pleasure in activities that used to provide enjoyment

> lack of/reduction in observable physical energy, stamina, resilience, reactivity
>
> lack of mental attention/focus
>
> difficulties sleeping
>
> either moving more slowly or becoming more physically agitated than is typical of the individual
>
> may have no more interest in food and start to lose weight from lack of eating
>
> contrarily, may eat much more, and gain weight

While any of these signs can happen to any of us on any given day, in the depressed individual they interfere with usual daily activities and interactions over at least a two-week time span.

Bipolar Disorder is visible through an individual's extreme mood swings. An individual with bipolar disorder will be very likely to first display the signs of depression (one of the two 'poles') as described above, with its polar opposite, the manic phase, displaying as a euphoric or high-energy mood, combined with overconfidence or extremes in other emotions such as anger. The person in the manic phase of the cycle might be quite talkative, feel less need for sleep, and take risks unimaginable in the individual's depressed state — again, the 'polar opposite' of depression.

Causes

For major depression and bipolar disorder alike, there is no single cause. A range of environmental, psychological, biological factors come into play, such as:

- general chronic health issues such as vascular disease, diabetes, arthritis, cancer, Parkinson's disease, etc.
- medication interactions or drug abuse
- genetic factors
- personality factors (overly sensitive; hair-trigger angry reactivity)
- stresses and how the individual deals with them (or cannot)
- major bereavement from loss of a loved one, which downcycles into long-term major depression

Treatments

A blend of self-treatments, self-initiated changes in lifestyle, and professionally facilitated treatments are effective for depressive disorders.

Lifestyle habit changes might include: exercise from aerobic and anaerobic approaches, chi gung or tai chi; mood-lifting music therapy from singing or playing in instrument or listening to music; journaling; self-directed computer aided therapy.

Professional interventions include: psychological interventions such as cognitive behavior therapy or CBT; problem-solving therapy; a structured life review with a therapist; anti-depressant medications after psychological assessment; family therapy; etc.

Anxiety

Anxiety disorder of any type is not unique to the elderly by any means, and can emerge at any age, although it often has its roots and early appearance in younger years.

Anxiety is feelings of fear, anxiousness or nervousness, irritation/irritability, impatience or feeling on edge, anger, worry, stress. It is an unpleasant state, whatever the degree of anxiety is experienced. Indeed, it can range from a mild worry that persists to an outright panic attack that paralyzes the mind and body.

Signs/symptoms of anxiety:

- It presents through the named feelings, certainly, but not in this way alone.

- Anxiety can also present through thoughts — the mind either racing as in nervousness or worry, or empty as in a panic attack.

- Behaviors are also an expression of anxiety: obsessive/compulsive behaviors (OCD), visible distress in or avoidance of certain types of situations, inability to sleep peacefully, resorting to/increasing use of alcohol or other detrimental substances.

- Sweaty palms, racing heartbeat, more shallow or gasping breathing, dry mouth, body pains (stomach or muscular are common), shaking — all these and others are how the physical body will act/react to anxiety.

Though most individuals experience these feelings or signs throughout life as a matter of passing reactivity, when they are prolonged, severe and/or interfere with life's activities (work, relationships, sleep/rest) it becomes a mental health issue called anxiety disorder.

Causes

To a medical professional, anxiety disorders differ in type. Some types, and potential causes:

- PTSD or post-trauma stress syndrome (known throughout history under different names, such as "shell shock" in active-duty soldiers), where the causative trauma is some event that is violent, frightening, causes injury (examples: wartime experiences, assault on one's person, involvement in violent accidents, etc.)

- Social phobia, where being with people causes anxiety

- Agoraphobia or fear of crowded or tight places

- Panic disorder, which is a shorter period of extreme and paralyzing anxiety, appearing inappropriate or unprovoked at the time, and which can reoccur unannounced at any time

Chapter 6: Identifying & Understanding Some Specific Mental Disorders

OCD or obsessive compulsive disorder, which includes obsessive (repetitive) thoughts as well as recurring/repetitive behaviors (examples: repetitive or prolonged hand-washing or organizing or cleaning)

GAD or generalized anxiety disorder, which is a prolonged state of anxiety affecting all/many areas of the individual's life activities.

Other causes are traumas during childhood or in the family unit, a family background of poverty, persistent fear of not being able to earn one's living or meet the bills, having an emotional sensitive personality, being trained to believe or otherwise perceiving the world (adults; males) to be threatening, etc. Some physical/medical conditions might also fragilize the individual and cause anxiety about being able to take care of oneself or even survive. Continual or prolonged anxiety experiences can lead to suicidal thoughts and behaviors.

Treatments

A blend of self-treatments, self-initiated changes in lifestyle, and professionally facilitated treatments are effective for depressive disorders.

Lifestyle habit changes might include: relaxation through massage, chi gung or tai chi; mood-lifting music therapy from singing or playing in instrument or listening to music; journaling; self-directed computer aided therapy.

Professional interventions include: psychological interventions such as cognitive behavior therapy or CBT;

problem-solving therapy; a structured life review with a therapist; anti-depressant medications after psychological assessment; family therapy; etc.

Mental Confusion & Dementia

The single word 'confusion' is used in many contexts, to be sure. In the case of mental health *Mental Confusion* points to a poor alertness or attention capability, disorientation as to one's surroundings or in relation to time, unclear or illogical speech and/or inability to track a conversation (stay tuned in and comprehend), disconnection with current reality, impaired memory as regards more recent events, etc.

Dementia is not a specific disease. It is a term for the "impaired ability to remember, think, or make decisions that interferes with doing everyday activities. Alzheimer's disease is the most common type of dementia." Dementia is a progressive decline in cognitive abilities, which translates to reduced memory recall, ability to plan or carry out a task with focus, language capability.

Signs and symptoms of Dementia and Mental Confusion:

- memory loss, as in forgetting things more often than in prior years

- misplacing items or placing them in inappropriate places

- not tracking conversation, as in forgetting the first part of a dialogue by the time the dialogue ends difficulty finding one's words or completing sentences

trouble tracking routine tasks such as paying bills

reduced analytical judgment (which is why scammers and telemarketers target the elderly with success)

becoming lost while driving or walking

apathy or withdrawal from usual social life activities

lack of inhibition leading to inappropriate behaviors

mood swings.

This decline, expressed in any one or a combination of the above ways, begins very subtly and develops over years and even decades. This latter aspect — developing over decades of one's life — is likely why we most often associate dementia with an elderly population.

Causes

Dementia is not a specific disease, and has many causes. In fact, other diseases may lead to dementia:

Alzheimer's disease is the most common underlying disease leading to dementia. Vascular cognitive impairment is also called vascular dementia. It might be due to a major stroke, a number of smaller strokes or any disease affecting blood vessels in the brain. Vascular cognitive impairment often goes hand-in-hand with Alzheimer's disease. (https://www.cdc.gov/aging/aginginfo/alzheimers.htm#Who)

There are also genetic factors underlying dementia. Brain injury which is severe enough to make the individual unconscious might increase risks for it later dementia. Chronic physical conditions such as high blood pressure/hypertension, high cholesterol, type 2 diabetes, obesity, and smoking can potentially lead to dementia.

Treatment

Dietary and lifestyle choices help prevent dementia, and these are personal behaviors, habits and routines to begin at any age (since dementia evolves and develops over years). As always, the earlier you start, the better.

Diet: Minimizing animal products for their unhealthy saturated and trans fats, and increasing plant-based eating is a good start.

Supplementation with vitamin E or B12 and multiple vitamins (without iron or copper) should be directed by the physician, as well as appropriate herbal supplements (example: gingko biloba) may be helpful.

Regular aerobic exercise should become a habit 3 to 5 times a week, such as swimming, cycling or brisk walking.

Lifelong and continuous cognitive stimulation should become a habit: It might take the form of ongoing learning or teaching, doing word games and puzzles and the like.

Psychological interventions when challenging behaviors appear. Mental health practitioners can help the individual identify triggers and find strategies to manage them.

Psychosis

Psychosis is a <u>general</u> term. It refers to a mental and behavioral state in which the person has lost touch with reality, and represents severe disruption in emotional, mental and behavioral functioning.

Schizophrenia, bipolar disorder, depression, delirium — in other words, other mental illnesses — can all lead to psychosis.

Schizophrenia

Signs and symptoms of schizophrenia

    delusions/false beliefs

    hallucinations/false perceptions, including hearing voices or seeing, feeling, tasting what is not there

    cognitive difficulties, such as problems concentrating or reasoning

    loss of motivation even for self-care

    withdrawing socially

    muted/blunted or other inappropriate emotional expression

Delirium

As a cause of psychosis, delirium can present and change very rapidly. It affects levels of alertness and consciousness, one's degree of awareness of surroundings and one's self-awareness.

Causes of psychotic disorders
- depression
- bipolar disorder
- cognitive dysfunction
- poor health, visual impairment
- negative stressful life events which trigger a psychotic episode

Treatment

Self-treatment is not an option, as one can determine from the expression of the disorder in the individual. Thus, it is advisable to consult trained mental health and medical professionals as one's first and best option for care and treatment.

- Consultation with a specifically-trained mental health professional — for assessment, treatment, review of progress
- anti-psychotic medications, prescribed after a thorough assessment, and monitored over time for effectiveness
- beneficial changes when possible in the personal environment of the affected individual
- other therapeutic/facilitated interventions to handle/manage extreme or aggressive behaviors

CHAPTER 6: IDENTIFYING & UNDERSTANDING SOME SPECIFIC MENTAL DISORDERS

Substance Abuse Disorders

A number of national population surveys have found that about half the people who experience a mental illness during their lives will also experience a substance use/abuse disorder and vice versa.

Substance use/abuse co-exists with anxiety disorders such as generalized anxiety disorder, panic disorder, and PTSD (post-traumatic stress disorder). Conversely, substance use/abuse disorders co-occur at high incidence with mental disorders, such as depression, bipolar disorder, attention-deficit hyperactivity disorder (ADHD), psychotic illness (severe mental disorders causing abnormal thinking and perceptions, losing touch with reality; two main symptoms are delusions and hallucinations), borderline personality disorder and antisocial personality disorder.

Patients with schizophrenia (a psychotic illness) have higher rates of alcohol, tobacco, and drug use disorders than the general population.

Suicide

Suicide is the taking of one's own life. Suicide is the harshest indicator of the presence of mental distress.

Drug overdoses took 70,000 American lives in 2017. Do these count as suicides? 7% of the American adult population suffered at least one major depressive episode in 2017. While this may not be a dependable precursor to suicide or even suicidal thoughts, it is a strong indicator of mental illness and mental distress in our population.

When we are speaking in medical terms, the general public is sometimes surprised to learn that substance use/abuse disorders, chronic anxiety, and suicidality are considered mental/behavioral illness issues.

Environmental factors matter a lot. This is what we might call 'life circumstances' and stressors. Stressors from the outside combine with internally generated stress. One's financial position may be a major stressor:

- the increasing cost of medical and preventive health care on the family budget
- the lack of savings in most American households
- the lack or the difficult access to physical and mental health treatment and services
- less income, unreliable income in elder years

Technology is a great stressor. Though our younger generations don't like to admit it, use of technology comes with great expectations, even for elders:

- everyone is 'digitally connected'
- everyone is on social media daily
- everyone is following along with the trends whatever they may be

Outside or societal stressors run the gamut from safety and security in one's neighborhood/home — indeed, guns and firearms are prevalent everywhere, and are used in half of all suicides — to the need for transportation to access any products or services.

Substance use and abuse is present at all ages and likewise runs the gamut from cigarettes (tobacco addiction), hard street drugs and more than one prescribed pharmaceutical drug.

Internal stressors are those thoughts such as, "I'm not keeping up", "I'm worried about _____", "I can't do it alone", "I'm so lonely", etc. Feelings run from worry, fear, anxiety, grief and depression, to anger and rage/outrage. Negative feelings and emotions entwine with negative outcomes in the health and wellness of the body, in a spiraling cycling effect.

Self-Quiz

True or False?

1. ____ Depression is not a mental illness. It is always just a 'passing thing'.

2. ____ Bipolar disorder used to be known as 'manic-depression'.

3. ____ Anxiety is a mental disorder made of feelings of fear, anxiousness or nervousness, irritation/irritability, impatience or feeling on edge, anger, worry, stress.

4. ____ PTSD (post trauma stress syndrome) and OCD (obsessive compulsive disorder) are both two forms anxiety disorder can present.

5. ____ Anyone with mental confusion could just be experiencing a momentary lapse of focus or processing capability, and this is not always a sign mental illness.

6. ____ Alzheimer's Disease is a form of dementia.

7. ____ Dementia is a progressive decline in cognitive (or mental) abilities.

8. ____ Just like some chronic physical diseases (diabetes, cancer), mental illness also develops and evolves over many years, often decades.

9. ____ Making lifestyle changes early in life are an iron-clad guarantee that you won't develop any physical or mental illnesses.

10. ____ Substance use/abuse disorders, chronic anxiety, and suicidality are definitely considered mental illness issues and treatable as such.

11. ____ 'Psychosis' is a general term, referring to a mental and behavioral state in which the person has lost touch with reality. Psychosis represents severe disruption in emotional, mental and behavioral functioning.

12. ____ Substance use/abuse (street drugs; misuse/abuse of prescription medications; heavy tobacco use; alcoholism) have no connection or relationship to mental illness.

1.F 2.T 3.T 4.T 5.T 6.T 7.T 8.T 9.F 10.T 11.T 12.F

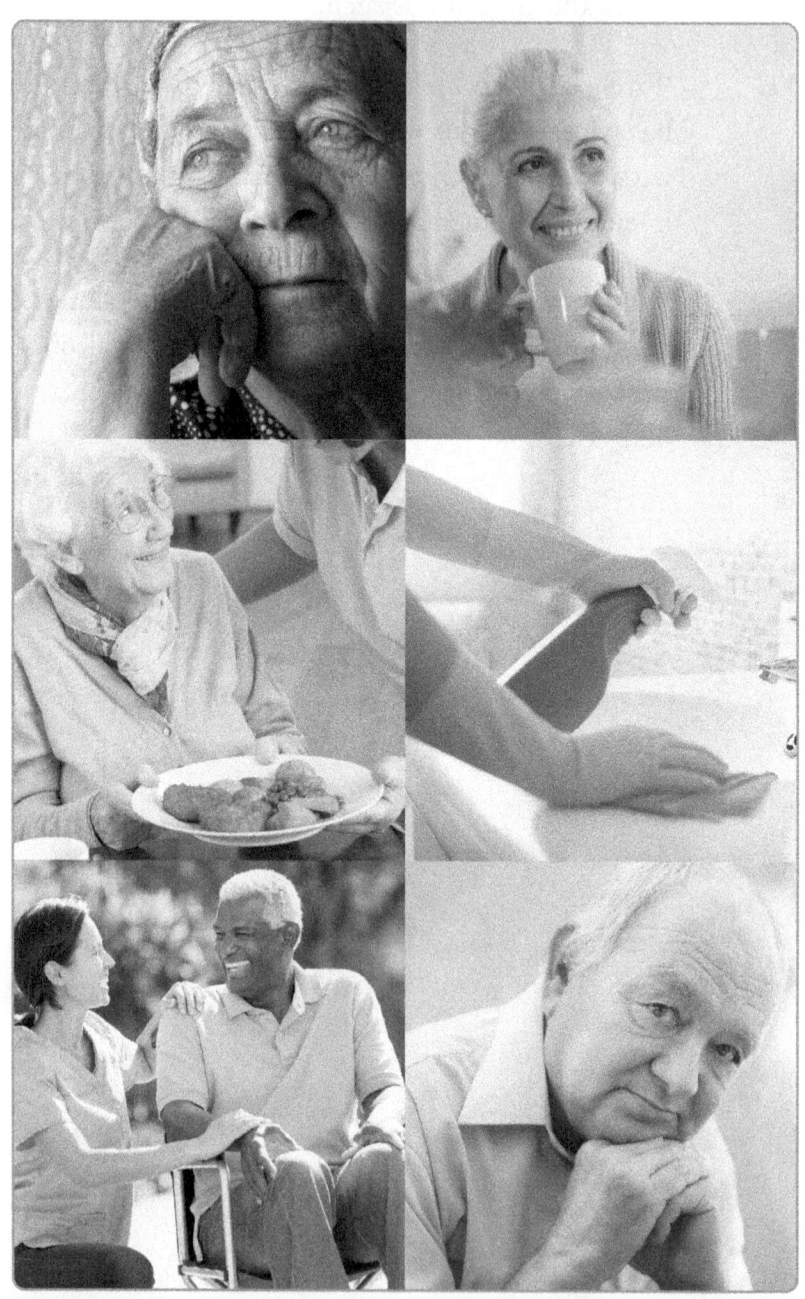

Chapter 7

SIX CASES

Case Study: How Health is a Holistic Achievement

his case study is an illustration of how physical health/illness/injury, emotions, and a change in independence and privacy are entwined with mental health matters in this elderly woman's case.

The elder

A previously mobile and independent, reasonably healthy 80-year-old lady prior to this accident, she had never married and had no children. She had lived independently and worked her entire life. Even after retirement from her main career, she developed a retirement activity serving others, which was very satisfying to her.

The accident

As a result of a fall, she had suffered a head trauma. Subsequently, she experienced major deterioration in most areas of functioning. To her, the most vexing was that she developed urinary incontinence. She was now in diapers.

The outcomes

Interestingly, her greatest new health worry was around her unaccustomed urinary incontinence. She saw that it led to a new lack of independence and very reduced privacy due to the intimate nature of care needed.

As she had been an independent woman until her accident, coping mechanisms were not in place. She found it now the tables were turned on her, as she was now is the one needing to be served and cared for.

From independence, she fell into a lack of self-esteem. From leading a private life, she fell into a need for physical and psychological care. From full control over her body, she fell into never quite knowing when she would need a restroom or if she would make it on time, or how to interact with her caregivers in rehabilitation.

The worry about her incontinence turned to anxiety. Her new lack of independence and privacy turned into with drawl and sadness, hopelessness and helplessness, a reduced self-esteem and self-image. Much of her anxiety was around her new need for care, paired with her perception that the staff didn't care to provide it (she had picked us up through the staff members' body language).

Mental health treatment plan

The plan was as much for the 80-year-old patient as for her caregivers.

The caregivers were informed to take their time and watch their body language (as they probably should have anyway, but the routine, the pressures and so on build up and we stop paying attention). They focused on her through eye contact, slow talking while also listening to her responses, and gentle touch.

In turn, the patient agreed to participate in small talk and conversation during care. She was reminded that she was fully able to process information for herself (that had not changed) and was encouraged to get information (about her condition, what further actions she could take for her own benefit, etc.) by asking questions until she understood the responses.

Mentally and intellectually, she came to agree that she was now in a new environment with new rules. She came to accept her need for coping/adaptive mechanisms and learned adapting behaviors.

She understood better that she was still the person she'd been and her self-esteem rose and her depression and sense of "It's all over now" lifted. She engaged more with the people around her. Physically, she no longer hesitated to drink needed fluids (the need to stay hydrated was made clear to her) in spite of the incontinence. Her appetite returned as well.

Case — Physical Decline, Loss of Independence

Not all elders experience mental illness as they age. Lest you believe I have forgotten about physical declines, here are some cases with examples of how local organizations' programs helped. They illustrate the dire need of elders for outside support, if only to set up non-medical care that allows them to remain in their own homes as long as possible.

There are always private and public organizations prepared to guide you and your loved ones to the support and care you require to continue living independently. If you have doubts about where to start, call your mental health care professional for resources near you.

Case — Food

The elder

She was living alone and found she could no longer physically leave the home to shop for food. Her cupboards were literally bare. Her financial resources were also extremely reduced.

Intervention from a local social services agent discovered that her financial abilities would not be sufficient to feed herself even if she could leave home to shop.

The outcome

The social services agent set her up on the regional low income subsidy program for food stamps. Meals on Wheels (home delivery of one meal a day) existed locally, and she signed up for that as well.

Other programs were found that kicked in to support her for her prescription medication out-of-pocket expenses and in-home medical assistance needs. All of this allows her to stay in her own home and maintain her independence.

Case — Taking Care of the Home

The elder

This 75-year-old female had gradually become quite physically frail from chronic diabetes, hypertension and high cholesterol. Her diabetes had resulted in dramatic visual impairment though not blindness.

Her Medicare took care of her medical care expenses. Her Social Security stipend took care of her other expenses. She had already signed up for to a subsidized group meal program at a location near home and continued to go there via public transportation. It was determined that the meal program met her daily nutritional needs.

The biggest risk

Her loss of physical mobility prevented her from taking care of things around the house. The condition of her home (cleanliness, safety, neatness — which also affects safety) had deteriorated in many ways. This was found to be the biggest risk factor to her being able to stay in the home and to stay safely there.

The outcome

After a visit from local social services (called in by a knowledgeable family member), the analysis of her needs and her ability to meet them resulted in keeping her in her home with the sole addition of subsidized housekeeping assistance every week.

She remains physically able to continue to travel for her daily meals and does so. Her family is making sure they stay in touch in case that ability changes, and have even spoken to a local version of the Meals on Wheels program for food delivery when she will need it.

Case — Loss of Income and Insurance Coverage

<u>The elder</u>

A 63-year-old married man suffered a stroke leaving him unable to walk. Being just a bit too young to qualify for Medicare, and not being able to work nor benefit from his company's insurance any longer, his wife quit her own job to care for him. Thus, the couple lost their second income and all medical insurance coverages.

<u>The outcome</u>

They applied for and received food stamps from their state program. Due to their dramatic drop in cash income, the program representative also informed them they qualified for state-paid medical insurance and some cash income (welfare benefits).

Although they shared some embarrassment and a bit of initial resistance at being 'on the dole' after a lifetime of caring for their own needs, it was a relief.

The spouse was also eligible for long-term care through various local non-profit programs after screening and assessment was completed. This included in-home respite care (a caregiver taking over for a few hours a week so that his spouse could relax and get away, do something else for a break).

Case — Depression Therapy

The patient

30 years ago, in his mid-30s, and over 14 or 15 months, he lost seven family members, friends or close acquaintances. Seven deaths in less than a year and a half of people he loved.

He was physically very healthy, but as he had barely digested and released the death of one friend, the death of the next one was upon him. He couldn't keep up emotionally. He fell into a deep, deep depression and it wouldn't quit. It was his first experience with such a thing.

Little did he know (but learned several years later) that his closer friends and family members were ringing their hands and saying amongst themselves, "Why doesn't he get some medical help?" (He says today, "Why they didn't tell me this directly I will never know.")

For nearly 2 1/2 more years, a loss of appetite led to falling under his healthy weight; he couldn't keep up at work; his very active social and sex life fell to nothing. It was isolation that felt most comfortable to him.

He did end up taking the bull by the horns himself, with no additional knowledge or education about depression. He just intuitively changed his environment — and quite radically.

He moved literally halfway around the world to a new culture and changed professions from education to hotel management.

The climb out of depression wasn't instant by any means. But the need to fend for himself in a new culture, get into the flow of a new profession and industry, and deal with strangers coming up to him for responses and solutions gradually pulled him up and out of it.

He later came upon an 'emotional release' methodology, and learned and uses it to this day.

Now in his mid-60s, he does know more about mental health and depression such as he experienced it back then. He does know what sort of help is available. But he also knocks on wood, hoping he's taking the right steps to keep himself from any future dive into depression or other mental disorder.

What he has to say to anyone around a depressed individual is this: *They can't help themselves. They don't have the energy or the motivation to do so. And probably not the information, either. Take him gently by the arm, make the appointment, go with him to it, get him started, and just keep on loving him.*

*Practical Approaches for First Aid
and Later Interventions*

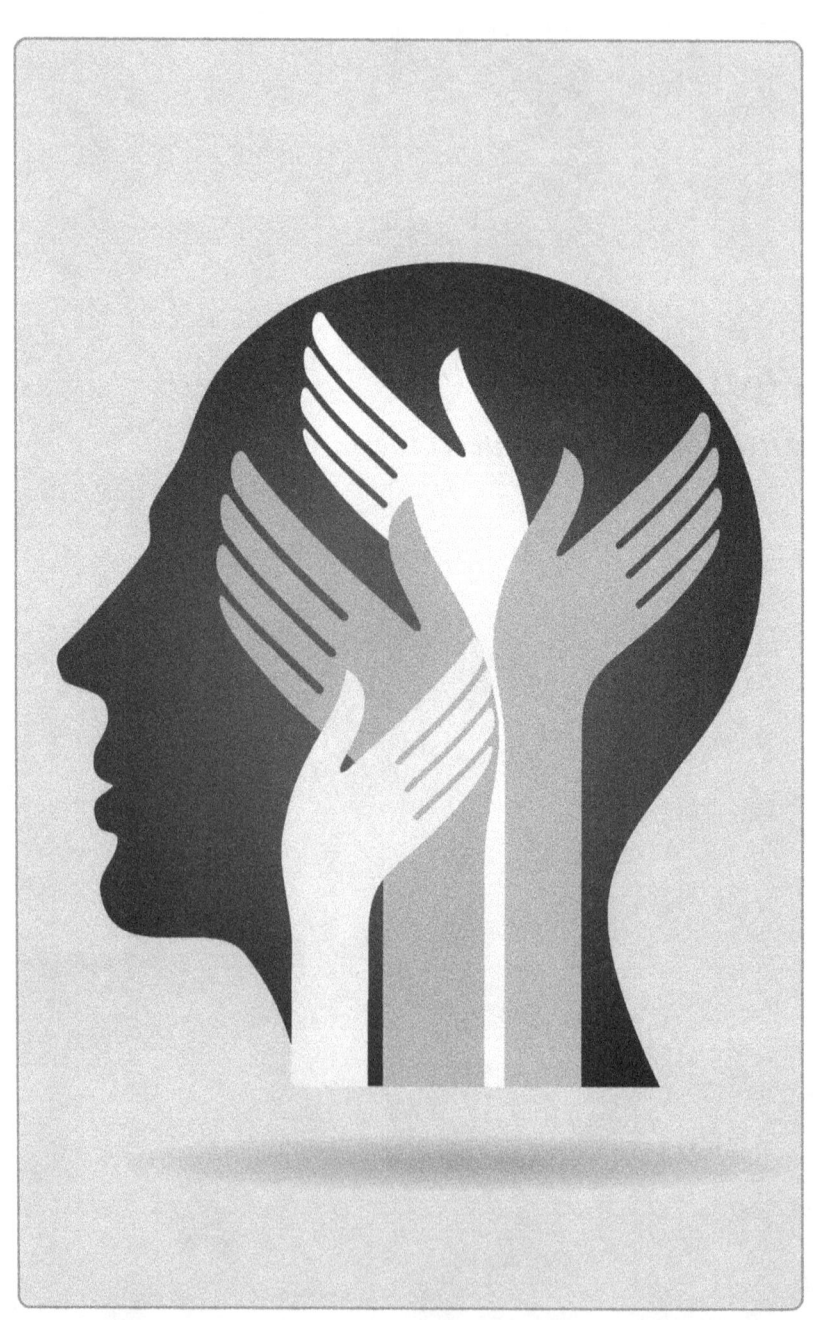

WHAT YOU CONTROL

he MacArthur Study Of Successful Aging found that experts are now shifting their research from illness to wellness. We are finding that, as in chronic physical disease, we can make some personally controlled lifestyle/behavioral changes to move towards greater mental health ... just as personal choices and actions within our control can move us out of a physical illness.

This is based on the fact that there are some effective things we can do for ourselves and for an elder we are caring for, and they are totally within our own control. We just need to decide to take these actions.

It is, however, also a fact that there are some aspects of our physical and mental health and wellbeing that are outside our control.

Myth: "It's genetic and we cannot do anything about our genes."

Reality: Genetics accounts for only about **1/3** among all factors determining or preventing health (mental and physical) as we age.

Myth: "It's very polluted where we live, there are tens of thousands of toxins in the air and in products we bring into our homes to clean and maintain them ... and if they're going to make us sick, there's nothing we can do about it."

Reality: Where you live can be a choice. What products you use in your home to clean it and in your garden to grow your plants is your choice. There are numerous non-toxic solutions today. Get informed and make a change.

Myth: "My family is not supportive. I have no other support."

Reality: If you don't state clearly what the new aging paradigm is for you, and don't state what you need because of it — you'll never know your family's position. Also, openness to seeking out support out in the community may just wake up your family to their negligence and/or internal capabilities!

What we can control, and what we cannot.

If genetics are only **1/3** of the equation as we saw above, what is in the other **2/3**? It is good news, because everything else is within our personal control. It turns out that creating health as you age is a collection of actions and habits you can change (or continue, when you are already doing one or more of them) — you are in charge of the change.

What Is In Your Control

☑ Social and Family Stigma

Yes, this is within your control. You can choose to change your own words and behaviors. You can change your thinking.

- The stigma on mental illness is a millennia-old belief pattern, but you can break it.

- Start by telling yourself that mental illness or decline is no different from physical illness, disease or increasing weakness. It's all one thing.

- Stop beating yourself up about it with self-stigmatizing.

- Stop guilt-tripping or shaming a loved one (after all, you *love* the person — and guilt and shame are not love).

- There is actually nothing "marginal" or "weird" about mental illness — no more strange than a broken leg, a case of pneumonia or an allergic outbreak.

- Recognize that there is treatment, education and healing care available. Seek it out, for yourself and for those you love. There is nothing shameful or embarrassing about getting professional care — not for a broken leg and not for acute chronic depression and suicidal thoughts (or any other mental disorder).

☑ Search For Local Resources

This too is in your control. Be creative. Think outside the box of traditional solutions.

- There are aid organizations within local, state, county, regional and federal government (example: the US counts well over 200 'welfare support' agencies of various kinds).

- There are non-profit organizations that directly provide the needed aid. Others specialize in being a clearinghouse (vetting agency) for all area aid options. Still others specialize in simply knowing the totality of area aid available, what type of aid they each offer and how/if you are eligible to receive any of that aid.

- There are faith-based aid organizations. Some run soup kitchens; participate in a Wheels-on-Meals type of meal delivery to their congregation's own people in need (elder and others). In those congregations, people of many skills and backgrounds gather and you can question them for inter-aid resources they know about and can guide you to.

- Question mental health professionals by calling their offices. They most often have lists to give you of available resource organizations and types of aid available.

Call the US Social Security Administration. There are several aid programs (SSI, etc.) for disabled or in-need individuals. And you don't already need to be of Medicare age (65+) to qualify.

☑ Positive Emotional Attitude

That is, an optimistic and positive outlook and approach to life versus a negative and pessimistic one.

Hint: the positive people survive 20 years longer than the latter, and in better overall health.

Lots of research points to longer and healthier life spans with a positive mindset.

Stress management and improved sleep are supportive ingredients of this positivity.

Declutter the spaces you live in. Make them safe and make them happy!

☑ Exercise

The adage about body mobility and responsiveness is true: *Use it or lose it.* Move your body.

You don't need to become a 'fitness club junkie', just do something you like.

Exercise outdoors when you can. Connecting with nature is soothing.

- Exercise with others when you can — at a club class or with the grandkids.

- Exercise — especially that gently-heart-pumping kind (aerobics) is not only good for physical health but for cognitive or mental health, lowering the risk of, and perhaps preventing, mental illnesses (research continues on this, but it makes common sense).

- Laugh, smile and have fun doing it!

☑ Brain-Training

This is the mental aspect of *'use it or lose it'*.

- Continuously use your brain, whether in later life intellectual work from a job you continue to successfully do, or a leisure-time brain training exercises such as crossword puzzles or chess on a daily basis. Doing so has been shown to protect your brain's health.

☑ Attention to Nutrition

This is a powerful choice in our personal control. More and more studies on the power of the food we eat to destroy health or created is being applied to mental health.

- What are you putting in your mouth? Is it Mother Nature's naturally grown food or factory processed junk?

Are you eating raw vegetable salads and raw fruit? Eating cooked is what we prefer, but raw produce holds water and we need the water!

Are you drinking enough water to be fully hydrated? The brain needs hydration and so does the rest of you.

We are what we eat, in all aspects of who we are — physical and mental, emotional and spiritual.

☑ Discover or Rediscover a Spiritual and Community Life

Interaction with one's inner spiritual faith and community of like-minded individuals also keeps us healthy in all sorts of ways. Connection with friends and family, who non-judgmentally support those changes you've decided to make.

> If you are new to any faith-based community, try it anyway. Maybe you have not attended since childhood. The faithful will tell you, "Welcome, it's never too late to join us."

> If you are a member of such a faith-based community, call upon its full resources. Church leaders and the spiritual leader (pastor, rabbi, imam, etc.) have connections, and will be able to provide you with names and addresses of resources that you can benefit from.

> Get and stay active in the congregation's activities. It represents on-going support of the human and the spiritual kind.

- If you have a hobby, don't give it up! Join groups of others who love it too. Chat, compare notes, learn and teach.

☑ Be Open to Medical and Mental Health Care and Assessments

- This includes not only openness to direct consultations but to pharmaceutical medication approaches when appropriate.

- A personal and family willingness to consult medical and mental health professionals at the earliest date possible.

- It is always better to know than not know — from a science/evidence-based 'lab results' and 'testing' perspective, and from an emotional/intellectual educational support perspective.

☑ Get a Buddy for Appointments

If you are the supporter of the elder needing care, you must realize that mental conditions can make it very frightening to even consider going to a mental health professional for a consultation and further guidance.

- Consider accompanying the elder (or get someone to go with you if the consultation is for you), and stay in the consultation together.

> This provides the comfortable presence of someone known, and provides you with a '2 heads are better than 1' approach to questioning the practitioner, sharing symptoms and circumstances with him (so nothing is forgotten) and for comparing notes together with your loved one later.

☑ Be Open to Making Some Changes

No one can change your personal habits and behaviors in your place.

> Such changes may be suggested by a professional or by common sense in view to preserving and regaining health.

> Most of us, young or older, never learned the self-care lessons of how to eat well, think well, be well. It is never too early to start. Get informed now.

> It is never too late to learn. Willingness to make lifestyle and behavioral changes is in your total control.

> The challenge of making lifestyle and behavioral changes is real. There is much support, however, and you can find an approach that works for you.

☑ Love Yourself and Love the Afflicted Elder

Love and compassion are powerful healers!

Do or Don't?

AMI, or the National Alliance of Mental Illness, helps caregivers and family members living with a mentally ill person with some Do's and some Don'ts. You will find many of these in previous chapters of our book, so look at this as a summary guide of intervention. Naturally some are very common sense based. Others are less natural to us.

Do:

- ☑ First Do No Harm. 'Primum Non Nocere' in the Latin. This is every physician's oath, and should be yours as well.

- ☑ Do keep the individual physically safe — to the degree you can.

- ☑ Do choose a familiar and private place/space to talk together.

- ☑ Do choose a quiet time — few/no interruptions or distractions.

- ☑ Don't be confrontational, judgmental or sound or look exasperated — it is not about you and your stresses.

- ☑ Do ease into any conversation about the person's issues.

- ☑ Do use a light conversational tone, and take it slow, simple and gradual.

- ☑ Do use the correct terminology (as provided by the person's doctor or therapist).

- ☑ Do be respectful, compassionate and empathetic to their context, condition and feelings about it.

- ☑ Do be a good listener. Do be responsive and make eye contact with a sincerely caring approach.

- ☑ Do ask them appropriate questions — on topic and easy to understand.

- ☑ Do give them the opportunity to talk and respond to you. Take your time.

- ☑ Do speak simply and in clear terms at all times.

- ☑ Do be aware of a person becoming confused by or distracted from your conversation with them. Let it go and try later.

- ☑ Do show respect and understanding for how they describe and interpret their symptoms.

- ☑ Do intervene if and when you are sincere - or don't go there.

- ☑ Do offer your support - but only if you can. Do ask, "How can I help?" if appropriate, or even, "Can I pray with you now?", or "Can I call someone for you?" if appropriate.

- ☑ Do always give the person hope for recovery by always offering encouragement to see a professional or to continue therapy / medication that has been prescribed.

Don't:

- ☒ Don't ever try to diagnose, 'therapize' or administer unknown drugs/substances to the individual.

- ☒ Don't step in if you yourself are not calm and able to think clearly.

- ☒ Don't show hostility — if you are not calm and non-judgmental, this type of intervention is not one you should undertake.

- ☒ Don't make jokes about their condition.

- ☒ Don't patronize them or act condescending in word or behavior. This communicates that you believe them to be stupid or inferior to you in some way, or that you do not believe their condition is serious. It is not about you or your opinion.

- ☒ Don't assume anything. Prepare with resources/information to truly help. Ask questions. Stay/be informed.

- ☒ Don't assume they want to 'pray on it' with you. Don't tell them to 'just pray and things will turn around'.

- ☒ Don't criticize, blame or rant.

- ☒ Don't raise your voice at the person.

- ☒ Don't be flip, cynical, sarcastic.

- ☒ Don't get upset at their upset!

- ☒ Don't beat around the bush when they ask you a direct and clear question. Speak in a straightforward and clear way, with the correct terms. If you are not the one to provide the answer (because you don't know it), say so.

- ☒ Don't be defensive yourself — it is not about you.

- ☒ Don't express your personal judgments or big emotional reactions — again, it is not about you.

- ☒ Don't just dive in to a long talk. Prepare. Observe.

- ☒ Don't talk *at* them. Carry on a quiet, calm two-way conversation, a dialog.

Now let's put these recommendations into a GAME PLAN™ for assisting those in need of support.

Self-Quiz

Review the above Do and Don't statements. Prioritize the top five of each — that is, the top 5 Do and the top 5 Don't statements — in order of highest importance. This will not mean the others are not important. It is simply going to be a reminder for you of what you (given your background and tendencies and personality) need to pay attention to in providing assistance to someone in crisis.

Top 5 Do Statements

1. _____
2. _____
3. _____
4. _____
5. _____

Top 5 Don't Statements

1. _____
2. _____
3. _____
4. _____
5. _____

Chapter 10

Your *GAME PLAN*™ for Assisting Others in Distress

oving from independence to interdependence (or straight into full dependency on others) is never an easy transition. An aging individual's top concern is retaining/losing his or her independence and privacy. But perhaps the shift should be viewed as moving from autonomy to <u>adaptability</u>. It is often not just the elder, but the entire family, needing to adapt to a 'new normal'. Moving from full control and autonomy to dependence means that the individual counts more on his strengths than on his (new) weaknesses.

Following the steps in this **GAME PLAN**™ gives you a good framework from which to assist virtually anyone, of any age, in moments of distress or mental health crisis.

GAME

- **G - Growth** - Help elders flourish in a mentally healthy environment. Life — and its opportunities for growth, experiences, learning — does not stop at any age.

- **A - Awareness** - Know the signs/symptoms for identifying a mental health issue or crisis. Be observant, as the elder may not recognize his need, or be unwilling to express it.

- **M - Match** - Match the elder with the best available resources. These include medical, home support, transportation, financial needs and so on.

- **E - Enquire** - Provide a short-term follow up to make sure needs are adequately met. If not, why not? If needs were not correctly assessed, make adjustments.

PLAN

- **P - Prepare** - Prepare for extended needs or accommodations. Needs evolve and responses to them can be planned.

- **L - Life/work balance** - Provide resources for family members, so that it is not over-extended. Provide for the elder's own self-care so there is as much self-sufficiency and independence as possible.

- **A - Assess** - Initial assessments may evolve, so regularly check on progress and new needs.

CHAPTER 10: YOUR GAME PLAN™ FOR ASSISTING OTHERS IN DISTRESS

N - Network - Maintain and improve the elder's social network and medical/home support networks. No one individual can do it all, even when it is the best-intentioned family member.

GAME PLAN™

Growth

Awareness

Match

Enquire

Prepare

Life/Work Balance

Assess

Network

Chapter 11

MYTH OR REALITY?

We have defined specific mental illnesses and its risk factors and some of the causes and treatments of them. We have discussed the stigma surrounding mental illness.

Connected in a real way to the stigma (and serving to perpetuate it) are *myths* about mental illness. A myth is 'a widely held, but false, belief about something'. To help you examine your own beliefs a bit deeper, look seriously at the following myths — and the facts to take to heart, because they turn those myths upside down.

Myth:

This is believed about depression and anxiety: "There's nothing wrong with you. It's all in your head," followed by saying, "Just make a decision to be well and snap out of it."

Fact:

If you are experiencing something different from your own personal 'normal', there is indeed something wrong. You might not understand what is wrong. You may not understand the triggers or causes, and therefore cannot snap out of it on your own.

Just as when you develop a physical pain in a specific area of the body, you know that something is wrong, and though you may not know what is wrong or how to fix it, you can consult a professional for advice. Start with your general practice doctor, who may send you on to a mental health doctor (psychiatrist or other).

Mental health professionals are trained in discovering the causes/triggers of the mental disorder and in developing appropriate treatments for them.

Myth:

This is often believed of individuals with depression, anxiety/panic attacks, bipolar disorder: "You say you have a mental illness, but in fact you're only lazy, crazy or just plain dangerous."

Fact:

Depression and anxiety have causes. They have triggers. This has been demonstrated time and again as fact. The causes and triggers are not something the person just 'chooses' so that they can 'get out of work' or stay isolated.

Even patients in psychiatric wards are rarely violent; all ward nurses and practitioners know this. Violence from mental disorders is just as rare as (or, otherwise stated, only as common as) violence in the general healthy population.

Myth:

A common belief is: Cognition and especially one's memory just declines with old age, and that's how it is. With chronic (repeated) memory lapses, you'll tease yourself or someone else, "You're just having one of those senior moments, ha ha!"

Fact:

Not all elders experience cognitive or memory decline. The statistics in the early part of this book support this fact.

Myth:

The common belief is: Psychiatry is not 'real' medicine. The belief is the psychiatrists never cure anyone, and that their diagnoses — much less their treatments — are not reliable most of the time.

Fact:

These mental health professionals' diagnoses are just as reliable as those made by other physical health professionals. Like physicians caring for your physical health, mental health practitioners understand that each person presents individual contexts to be understood to get to the root cause(s) and/

or triggers. Thus, all doctors are really like 'detectives' and 'investigators'.

They are trained to discover the entire context of the mental disorder (identifying all of the environmental and all of the physical health issues; identifying multiple mental health issues).

Keep in mind that two psychiatrists will differ in opinion just as often as two medical doctors in another specialization. That is where the phrase "get a second opinion" comes from!

Myth:

We all share, to some degree, the belief (or the hope?) that, "Mental illness will never affect me. I'm generally healthy, so I don't need to concern myself with that type of illness either."

Fact:

One in four Americans will deal with depression each and every year. Since it's not the <u>same</u> people affected every year, chances are it will affect you at some point in your life.

We experience a number of major and minor **_stressors_** throughout life. None of us — even the healthiest, even the most care-free among us — are immune to such stresses. They include life events such as

- loss of a spouse or other very close loved one and that grief loss of a job and the distress, anxiety, depression and stress it causes (especially when the job loss is at an older age, when we are typically less desirable as new employees to a new employer)

moving house for whatever reason

getting married

getting a divorce or separating from a long-time partner/spouse

dealing with some violence or crime; being subject or perpetrator on one and dealing with the aftermath/consequences

dealing with a personal illness or injury that takes focus to heal from

retiring, leaving the world of daily work routines and making those adjustments

Other grave disappointments can come our way during our lives — they all potentially lead us to or through a major depression, anxiety or other mental health disorder which can only benefit from professional diagnosis and treatment.

Recognizing Trigger Points

Discussion of stress is a good time to look more closely at triggers. Some we create ourselves. Others come from our environment.

Triggers for mental/behavioral illness are often the equivalent of stressors. They are not always a tipping point, in that many people have strong coping mechanisms they can call upon, but they need attention. Some triggers include:

- Alcohol, tobacco or substance use/abuse

- Change of environment, like moving into an assisted living facility or into a child's own home or being abandoned by family when the last adult child moves away from the family home

- Losing a long-time spouse late in your shared life

- Terminal illness of a loved one (deep bereavement can set in even before the loved one's death)

- One's own long-term illness (e.g., cancer, diabetes or heart disease)

- Medication interactions and/or too many drugs

- Physical disability

- Physical illnesses that can affect emotion, memory and thought

- New or sustained poor diet, malnutrition, undernutrition

- Chronic dehydration

Myth:

We believe (once we've heard about someone's mental illness diagnosis or that he/she is getting some therapy or other mental health treatment) that, "People with mental health issues fall apart at each new stress, have a low tolerance for change, and therefore cannot hold down a responsible job or perform well."

Fact:

With today's effective diagnoses and treatments, those with a mental illness soon find they can go back to work and be just as productive as before, just as effective as other employees who are not dealing with any health issue.

Keep in mind that when a person is physically ill or has a chronic physical-body disease such as diabetes or cardiovascular disease, that person's productivity is affected as well… until appropriate treatment is underway and takes effect.

Likewise keep in mind that the above-named stressors do <u>not</u> necessarily result in a chronic mental disorder! When a co-worker is suddenly 'not himself' he may be dealing with or reacting to a stress at home (his child may be in trouble or his neighborhood may be seeing a rash of break-ins). So, at any time in your workplace you may see 'dips and bumps' in others' ability to cope which is passing.

Both <u>*mental and physical*</u> health issues can be treated — with treatment goal being to bring the individual back to full productivity and comfort at work and at home.

Myth:

The belief is somewhat related to cancer as viewed throughout most of the 20th century, and it is this: "Once you have contracted a mental illness, it's all over. It's no use getting treatment because you will never recover anyway." The belief is that "once contracted, forever doomed."

Fact:

Studies actually show that people with mental health disorders do get better and many recover completely with proper treatment.

Today with cancer — a physical disease — we talk about someone 'being in remission'. That means there is no remaining evidence of that cancer. Likewise in treatments for many mental disorders, and although we do not use the term that much, a patient can arrive at a state of 'remission'. The parallel is real. 'Recovery' from both physical and mental Illnesses means the patients have gone through treatment and a healing process which allows them to live, work, study and fully participate in life as they wish to.

Proper diagnosis is key and self-diagnosis is not really the best option. This said, you will know your own symptoms and how you have moved out of your 'normal' and into another state of being. Share it all with a professional who will then be able to connect them to a mental illness and appropriate treatment.

Myth:

The common belief is lack of control: "There's no way to prevent mental illness. When it's going to hit you, it hits you."

Fact:

The risk factors of mental illness are fairly well understood. 'Risk factors' are a blend of things within our control (use/abuse of drugs or alcohol or tobacco throughout life) and outside it (genetics).

Education about the risk factors, with right action and right lifestyle choices to lessen or eliminate them go a very long way to preventing mental illness from occurring and/or minimizing its impact on your life in later years.

Part 4

Your Own Healthy Aging

Chapter 12

PRACTICAL APPROACHES YOU CAN ADOPT

If you are in your 40s, 50s or 60s, and have thus far experienced great health — both mental and physical — that is great! But don't get complacent.

You have certainly already deduced that a number of the mental illness risk factors can be eliminated or minimized for yourself because they are under your direct control. What are you waiting for?

Humans are creatures of habit — in fact, our daily lives run about 70% (if not more) on routine actions and behaviors, routine thoughts and emotions. I would agree, if from nothing more than my personal experience and observation of many elder patients, that we are all somewhat subject to that lifetime habit that seems to be 'carved in stone'. But there is hope! We don't have to 'run on automatic'. When those habits and routines no longer serve us, we have control. We can make changes. We can drop the old in favor of healthy new habits.

The areas to look after are no surprise, and you need to pay attention to them all, as they represent a whole — a holistic, balanced approach to wellness and well-being:

- Physical health
- Mental health
- Spiritual health
- Social health
- Emotional health

Heart disease, diabetes and cancer are three top killers of the body in our society. Mental disorders, while not always a killer in the literal sense, does indeed 'kill' the ability or desire to live a full and satisfying life.

I mention those chronic diseases here, and though you may protest that the physical health of the body is not the topic at hand, but only mental health, we are a *holistic organism*. What the body suffers, so does the brain and the mind. What the mind or the brain suffer, so will the body. The entwined nature of our mental, emotional, physical aspects must not be ignored. It is all interconnected, say what you will!

What We Eat and What We Think

I have noticed that my colleagues in, particularly, Cardiology, Oncology (cancers) and Diabetes specializations are moving to nutrition as a major lifestyle change that can (and indeed systematically does) improve and even heal the vascular blockages, insulin imbalances and cancer-cell-feeding that poor diet has created. What we put in our mouths is within our control and the research and data are showing more and more that it is crucial to eat correctly in order to create good physical health.

Common sense leads us to recognize that loads of sugar or loads of sodium/salt in our diets will create 'some kind of overload' in the body. An overload is an imbalance. Common sense tells us that eating 'real' food from Mother Nature, as opposed to the processed foods straight from a food factory, must (somehow) be better and healthier for us. But we ignore the evidence all too often in the name of convenience.

Likewise in psychiatry, we are gently moving more and more into the recognition that we are both what we eat and what we think. We extend the 'what we eat' aspect of things to include other ingestibles such as tobacco and street drugs (with their built-in brain-changing toxic chemicals), alcohol overuse/abuse (with its brain-changing effects). Alas, to that we must add that well-intended prescribed drugs, when too great in number, can interact if not 'toxically' with each other, still wreak some havoc on the body and brain's natural harmonious interactions.

We likewise take the research on positive/negative emotional patterns to heart to make a change towards a more positive outlook. Being positive has been clearly proven to move us into a place of independently managing/coping with life's stresses. Being negative leads us like a magnet to caving in to them, not coping well or at all, suffering much longer than we need to.

It has unequivocally been shown that positive people manage or cope better with the stressors of life than negative individuals; that positive individuals get physically sick less and heal faster and that negative emotions will both create and perpetuate physical illnesses.

Eating more healthfully — it is for physical, but also mental and emotional health. Thinking more positively likewise is for that holistic health. These are two 'habits' to replace the ones that no longer (if they ever did) serve your continuous holistic health.

Other Habits to Support Mental and Physical Health

You have seen the entanglement of mental, emotional and physical health issues in many of the discussed mental disorders. This is part of what makes mental illness — and correct, complete diagnosis — so individual and so challenging.

This said, many of these seemingly diverse illnesses share actions to take in their treatment, as you may have noticed. So many of the 'solutions' are non-medical and are 'preventative', that they serve as a foundation for new habits and routines for you to adopt to create 'healthy aging' for yourself.

Many therapies and treatments will include a blend of the following, and start now by adopting them into your own daily routine — for holistic health:

A. **Getting exercise**, and for the elderly this means in a safe environment (as elders fear falling or injuring themselves more than younger adults do). Outdoors is best; indoors will suit others better.

Some aerobic (the exercise that gets the heart pumping) and some muscle building (lifting weights) exercise several times a week might be a new habit — but a good one to develop for mental health.

Exercise to improve and maintain balance, spatial awareness and suppleness can be found in Tai Chi or Yoga. Such classes are taught around the world.

B. **Attention to nutrition** and right eating for health. This includes sufficient daily calories, sufficient quality of nutritional elements, enough water to be/stay hydrated.

There are frequent recommendations about fiber in food, and you get it through plant foods (virtually all of them have fiber), and not through animal foods (meat and dairy have no fiber).

C. **Keeping the brain/intellect active**. Mental health professionals call this 'cognitive intervention' — 'brain-training'.

Crossword puzzles, chess, Go, and other brain games are perfect brain trainers.

Memory, reasoning and processing speed training are also very successful in keeping cognition alert.

D. **Keeping one's social network** close. Being active with people of like interests, with people you love and care about goes a long way to remaining both emotionally and mentally healthy.

Connection with others through face-to-face conversation, shared activities, inter-aid (as in volunteering together in a community venture or non-profit mission) are common ways people stay connected.

Share meals with friends and family, and talk. Talk about and share hobbies together and learn from each other. If you have a specific skill or knowledge base, teach it to a younger generation. The connection is worth it.

E. **<u>Strong spiritual life.</u>** This is not about religion. Certainly for some, it will be. For others, another faith- or spiritually-based practice is what is deeply fulfilling. For yet others, it is sharing one's life philosophy with like-minded people.

F. **<u>Properly prescribed and administered pharmaceutical treatment.</u>** A psychiatrist is a licensed physician and may prescribe a drug treatment. As with all pharmaceuticals, the utmost obedience to the prescribed dosage (and length of time used) is required; tracking improvements (or lack thereof) with the prescribing physician is vital.

<u>NOTE</u>: Not all cases benefit from or improve with a drug therapy. The fact that a physician does not prescribe a drug is something you can be thankful for! All drugs have secondary (aka side) effects and are difficult to keep up by most patients. Be faithful to the prescription if one is given, but be glad if drug treatment is not called for!

Conclusion

Like our physical health, our mental or behavioral health — and how it unfolds over the years of our lives — is a dynamic phenomenon. Health and illness are, for most people, an ebb and flow, with periods of calm, healthy wellbeing and others of illness or imbalance.

Throughout our lives, we might be called on to assist others in a mental health crisis, in a period of emotional overwhelm, in a period of behavioral health challenges. You now have more information to help you face such needs in others, even though you never become a mental or behavioral health professional yourself.

Any one of us may require assistance for our own mental health issues. They can occur suddenly in reaction to one of life's many stressors, and resolve just as quickly. Or they may develop out of sight, grow in severity and require expert intervention and treatment.

But we are also cognizant of this fact: Much of our holistic health is in our own control, and by taking right action, exchanging some current unhealthy habits for some health-creating ones, we can minimize or eliminate our own risk factors associated with mental illness.

A portion of our health or illness is self-created, but not all. Within our control are most of our daily habits:

- What we eat (foods — health-building or health-depleting)
- Toxins we ingest (drugs, alcohol, tobacco)
- The thoughts we think
- The outlook on life that we choose (our positivity or negativity)
- Going towards or ignoring health

Some risk factors are outside our control (or our awareness). We sometimes cannot easily detect (or hope to change) such outside factors as:

- hidden toxicities in our environments
- the negativity of the people around us
- our unquestioned acceptance of false beliefs
- unhealthy habits we have taken too much for granted
- our genetic makeup

Conclusion

We are holistic beings. Not just a body. Not just a mind. Our physical, emotional, mental and behavioral aspects entwine, entangle and combine in ways unique to each of us. Knowledge, acted upon, is your personal power to heal and be healthy.

SOURCES

Chapter 1

1. "Successful Cognitive and Emotional Aging", case cited page 158, by Katzman et al, "Development of dementing illnesses in an 80-year-old volunteer cohort" published in Annals of Neurology, 1989.

Chapter 2

1. Lancet Commission On Global Mental Health, October 2018.

2. The CDC: Center for Disease Control and Prevention, (www.cdc.gov):
   https://www.cdc.gov/aging/data/index.htm
   https://www.cdc.gov/aging/pdf/state-aging-health-in-america-2013.pdf
   https://www.cdc.gov/aging/emergency/general.htm

3. World Health Organization:
   https://www.who.int/whr/2001/media_centre/press_release/en/
   https://www.who.int/ageing/publications/india/en/
   https://www.who.int/ageing/publications/global_health.pdf

4. NAMI, the National Alliance on Mental Illness:
   https://www.nami.org/learn-more/mental-health-by-the-numbers

5. National Institute on Aging:
   https://www.nia.nih.gov/health/depression-and-older-adults

Chapter 5

1. https://www.healio.com/psychiatry/practice-management/news/online/%7B321841f4-d996-49ca-8da8-152ae893263d%7D/stigma-reducing-campaign-may-urge-people-to-seek-mental-health-care

2. https://www.psychologytoday.com/us/blog/why-we-worry/201308/mental-health-stigma

3. https://www.ncbi.nlm.nih.gov/pmc/articles/PMC1489832/

4. "Stigma in Dementia: It's time to talk about it" Lori Harper PhD; Bonnie M. Dobbs PhD; Shana D. Stites, PsyD MS MA; Martha Sajatovic MD; Kathleen C. Buckwalter PhD RN FAAN; Sandy C. Burgener PhD RN FAAN

Chapter 6

1. National Institute on Drug Abuse -https://www.drugabuse.gov/publications/research-reports/common-comorbidities-substance-use-disorders/part-1-connection-between-substance-use-disorders-mental-illness

2. Center for Disease Control (https://www.cdc.gov/aging/dementia/index.html)

About the Author

DR. MURALI RAO is the Professor and Chairman of the Department of Psychiatry and Behavioral Neurosciences at Loyola University Medical Center in Chicago. He specializes in liaison and emergency psychiatry. Additionally, he serves as a member of multiple professional bodies including the American College of Psychiatrists, the Academy of Psychosomatic Medicine, CINP, the Indian Psychiatric Society, and the American College of Forensic Psychiatry.

Dr. Rao has received multiple awards and fellowships including Distinguished Life Fellow by the APA, Outstanding Academician Award by the Indo-American Psychiatric Association, and the Master Teacher Award by the Stritch School of Medicine. Dr. Rao has also had more than 50 journal publications.

www.ingramcontent.com/pod-product-compliance
Lightning Source LLC
Chambersburg PA
CBHW020258030426
42336CB00010B/821